THE PERFECTLY USELESS BOOK OF

USELESS
INFORMATION

THE PERFECTLY USELESS BOOK OF
USELESS
INFORMATION

*You'll Never Need to Know Anything That's in This
Book . . . But Read It Anyway*

DON VOORHEES

A PERIGEE BOOK

A PERIGEE BOOK
Published by the Penguin Group
Penguin Group (USA) Inc.
375 Hudson Street, New York, New York 10014, USA

Penguin Group (Canada), 90 Eglinton Avenue East, Suite 700, Toronto, Ontario M4P 2Y3, Canada
(a division of Pearson Penguin Canada Inc.)
Penguin Books Ltd., 80 Strand, London WC2R 0RL, England
Penguin Group Ireland, 25 St. Stephen's Green, Dublin 2, Ireland (a division of Penguin Books Ltd.)
Penguin Group (Australia), 250 Camberwell Road, Camberwell, Victoria 3124, Australia
(a division of Pearson Australia Group Pty. Ltd.)
Penguin Books India Pvt. Ltd., 11 Community Centre, Panchsheel Park, New Delhi—110 017, India
Penguin Group (NZ), 67 Apollo Drive, Rosedale, North Shore 0632, New Zealand
(a division of Pearson New Zealand Ltd.)
Penguin Books (South Africa) (Pty.) Ltd., 24 Sturdee Avenue, Rosebank, Johannesburg 2196, South
Africa

Penguin Books Ltd., Registered Offices: 80 Strand, London WC2R 0RL, England

While the author has made every effort to provide accurate telephone numbers and Internet addresses at
the time of publication, neither the publisher nor the author assumes any responsibility for errors, or for
changes that occur after publication. Further, the publisher does not have any control over and does not
assume any responsibility for author or third-party websites or their content.

Copyright © 2010 by Don Voorhees
Cover design by Bryan Landsberg
Text design by Tiffany Estreicher

First edition: May 2010

Library of Congress Cataloging-in-Publication Data

Voorhees, Don.
   The perfectly useless book of useless information : you'll never need to know anything that's in this
book . . . but read it anyway / Don Voorhees.—1st ed.
      p.   cm.
   ISBN 978-0-399-53587-1
   1. Curiosities and wonders.   I. Title.
   AG243.V666 2010
   031.02—dc22   2009053888

PRINTED IN THE UNITED STATES OF AMERICA

10   9   8   7   6   5   4   3   2   1

Most Perigee books are available at special quantity discounts for bulk purchases for sales promotions,
premiums, fund-raising, or educational use. Special books, or book excerpts, can also be created to fit
specific needs. For details, write: Special Markets, Penguin Group (USA) Inc., 375 Hudson Street, New
York, New York 10014.

This book is dedicated to all the millions of information junkies out there who can't get enough useless knowledge. Here's a little more!

CONTENTS

MASCOT MUSINGS

A squirrel nest is known as a "drey."

The largest squirrel on Earth is the Indian giant squirrel, which can grow to three feet in length.

The African pygmy squirrel is only about four inches long, including the tail.

A squirrel can use its tail as a "parachute" should it fall from a tree. The tail can also be used to cushion a hard landing and to communicate with other squirrels.

The largest concentration of squirrels in the United States is found in Washington, DC. Lafayette Park, across from the White House, is known as the "Squirrel Capital of the World."

Squirrel meat can be substituted for chicken or rabbit in recipes.

Squirrels have been kept as pets and are said to be as easy to train to do tricks as dogs.

Twiggy the Waterskiing Squirrel is a novelty act in which a squirrel has been trained to "water-ski" on two little foam "skis" behind a remote-control boat.

LET THE GAMES BEGIN

GO! NADS!

The Rhode Island School of Design hockey team is called the Nads. Their team cheer is "Go Nads!" The basketball team is the Balls. Their slogan is "When the heat is on, the Balls stick together."

Arizona's Scottsdale Community College's teams are known as the Fighting Artichokes.

Illinois's Teutopolis High School's teams are the Wooden Shoes.

The University of California Santa Cruz's mascot is the banana slug.

THE NEW YORK BORROS?

The New York Jets were almost named the "Borros," after the five boroughs. However, someone in the organization was wise enough to realize that many would call them the "jackasses" instead.

The Baltimore Ravens got their name because of the city's association with Edgar Allan Poe.

The Orlando Magic were nearly called the "Juice."

ON ICE

Sixty-eight percent of professional hockey players have lost at least one tooth.

The term "hat trick" was first used in cricket, not hockey, in 1858, when H. H. Stephenson received a hat for taking three wickets in consecutive balls. (Whatever that means.)

Former Chicago Blackhawk Bill Mosienko holds the National Hockey League record for the fastest hat trick, when he scored three goals in just twenty-one seconds against the New York Rangers on March 23, 1952.

THAT'S A LOTTA POINTS

Danny Heater, of Burnsville, West Virginia, scored 135 points in a high school basketball game on January 26, 1960.

In 1916, Georgia Tech beat Cumberland College 222 to 0, for the biggest blowout in college football history. John Heisman, for whom the Heisman Trophy would later be named, coached Georgia Tech.

HOMEMADE SPORTS

Ralph W. Samuelson invented water-skiing in 1922, when he steam-bent two eight-foot-long pine boards, strapped them on his feet, and was towed behind a motorboat on Lake Pepin, Minnesota.

Scott and Brennan Olson of Minnesota invented Rollerblades in 1980 when they took hockey skates and replaced the blade with three in-line wheels.

VROOOM!

The Indianapolis 500 is the world's largest single-day sporting event, with more than a half million spectators attending.

The gasoline-powered engines of NHRA Pro Stock cars produce approximately 1,200 horsepower. By comparison, the average new minivan has about 250 horsepower. The nitromethane-powered engines of NHRA Top Fuel dragsters and Funny Cars produce about 7,000 horsepower. These cars can go from 0 to 100 miles per hour in less than 0.8 second.

In 1955, during the 24 Hours of Le Mans, the car driven by Pierre Levegh flew into the crowd, killing him and eighty spectators. This was the most catastrophic accident in motor sports history.

DIAMOND IN THE ROUGH

Alexander Cartwright invented the first baseball field and the early rules of the game in 1845.

The first recorded baseball game was played in Hoboken, New Jersey, in 1846, between Alexander Cartwright's New York Knickerbocker Base Ball Club and the New York Base Ball Club (aka "the New York Nine"). The latter won the game 23–1 in four innings. Cartwright served as umpire and imposed a six-cent fine on players for swearing.

The basic layout of the baseball diamond has remained relatively unchanged since the original Knickerbocker Rules of the 1840s.

In early games, innings were one out, balls caught on one bounce were outs, and throwing the ball at base runners to make them out was legal.

Up until 1884, pitchers had to throw the ball underhand.

Before 1893, pitchers threw from a square, known as a "box." They were allowed to get a running start in the box.

In the first college baseball game, played in 1859, Amherst defeated Williams 73–32, in twenty-five innings.

In 1929, the Yankees became the first team to use uniform numbers regularly (the Cleveland Indians had previously done so, but briefly). Numbers were assigned by the player's position in the batting order. Since Babe Ruth batted third, he was assigned 3. Lou Gehrig, who batted cleanup, was number 4.

BOYS OF SUMMER

Pittsburgh Pirates pitcher Doc Ellis claimed he was high on LSD when he threw a no-hitter against the San Diego Padres on June 12, 1970. Ellis was called in to pitch on short notice, after having taken the drug earlier in the day.

Satchel Paige was the oldest rookie in Major League Baseball history when he debuted with the Cleveland Indians in 1948, at the age of forty-two.

On April 23, 1999, Fernando Tatis, of the St. Louis Cardinals, who had never hit a grand slam in his career, hit two in the same inning, making him the only major leaguer ever to do so.

In 1938, at the age of eighteen, John Forsythe did the public address announcing for the Brooklyn Dodgers at Ebbets Field.

In a 1957 game, Philadelphia Phillies player Richie Ashburn fouled off a pitch that hit fan Alice Roth, breaking her nose. During the same at bat, Ashburn fouled another ball into the stands, again hitting Roth, as she was carted away on a stretcher.

In Major League Baseball, 1968 was known as "The Year of the Pitcher." In that year, the only American League player to hit over .300 was Carl Yastrzemski (.301).

SULTAN OF SWAT

George Herman Ruth Jr. signed a contract to play with the then minor-league Baltimore Orioles in 1914. Since Ruth was only nineteen at the time, the others players called him "Babe." In 1919, Ruth hit twenty-nine home runs, more than any *team* did in the American League that year.

In 1920, Sam Vick became the only person ever to pinch-hit for Babe Ruth, after the Babe had hurt his hand earlier in the game. With the bases loaded, Vick tripled to drive in three runs.

PERFECTION

In 1917, Boston Red Sox pitcher Ernie Shaw threw a "perfect" game in relief of starter Babe Ruth. The Babe walked the game's lead-off batter and was ejected after arguing with and throwing a punch at the home plate umpire. The runner on first was thrown out stealing, and Shaw went on to retire the next twenty-six batters. It was considered a perfect game at the time, but the standards have since been revised.

In the history of Major League Baseball, there have been only eighteen perfect games pitched.

BY THE NUMBERS

Only thirteen major-league players have hit two grand slams in one game.

Fourteen major-league players have hit four home runs in one game.

There have only been fifteen unassisted triple plays in major-league history, all by first basemen, second basemen, and shortstops. There have been two game-ending unassisted triple plays—one in 2009 and one in 1927.

THE "RIGHT" POSITION

Due to the counterclockwise flow of the game of baseball, left-handed catchers are exceedingly rare. In fact, there have only been five left-throwing catchers who have played in one hundred or more Major League Baseball games and only one career catcher of eight hundred or more games—Jack Clements—who played from 1884 to 1900.

KNUCKLEHEADS

Phil and Joe Niekro are the most successful brother pitching combination in Major League Baseball history, with 539 wins between them. Both brothers specialized in the knuckleball. In 973 lifetime at-bats, Joe's only home run came off his brother Phil.

The first player to throw the knuckleball in professional baseball was probably Lew "Hicks" Moren of the Philadelphia Athletics, in 1906, although Eddie Cicotte of the Boston Red Sox is sometimes credited with its invention in 1908.

SPITTERS

Spitballs were made illegal in 1920, except for the sixteen pitchers who were already throwing them, who could continue to do so until they retired.

The spitball is partially blamed for the death of Ray Chapman, who was killed when a pitched ball hit him in the head. It is believed he couldn't see the ball since it was covered in chewing tobacco juice spit on it by the pitcher.

Before Chapman's death in 1920, only one baseball was used for the entire game. If the ball was hit out of the playing field, a team employee would retrieve it from the stands.

In 1921, a thirty-one-year-old stockbroker caught a foul ball at New York's Polo Grounds and refused to give it back. He was ejected from the game, sued the Giants, and won. Ever since then fans have been keeping these souvenirs.

THE GEORGIA PEACH

Ty Cobb's first name was Tyrus. He was nicknamed the "Georgia Peach" because he was born in Narrows, Georgia.

Ty Cobb's mother shot and killed his father after she mistook him for an intruder one day in 1905 when he appeared at her bedroom window trying to catch her in an act of infidelity.

Ty Cobb stole second base, third base, and then home in the same inning four different times in his career.

In 1909, Ty Cobb led the American League in home runs with nine, but never hit a ball over the fence. They were all inside-the-park homers.

CYCLONE

Cy Young was born Denton True Young. He picked up the nickname "Cyclone," later shortened to "Cy," during his minor-league pitching days, because of his blazing fastball.

One of Young's early major-league catchers, Chief Zimmer, would put a piece of steak inside his mitt to protect his hand from Young's fastball.

FAMILY AFFAIR

In 1987, Cal Ripken Sr. was the manager of the Baltimore Orioles and his sons Cal Jr. and Billy played together in the same infield.

Billy Ripken's 1989 Fleer baseball card showed him holding a bat with the words "fuck face" written on the knob.

In 1990, Cal Jr. only made three errors in 162 games at shortstop, a major-league record for best fielding percentage at his position.

BIGGEST WINNER *AND* LOSER

Cornelius McGillicuddy Sr. is better known as Connie Mack. He managed the Philadelphia Athletics for their first fifty seasons. He holds the record for most games won (3,731), as well as most games lost (3,948) and most games managed.

PEE WEE PLAYERS

Carl Stotz started Little League Baseball in Williamsport, Pennsylvania, in 1939, with three teams. Today, there are nearly 200,000 teams worldwide.

> Girls were first allowed to play Little League Baseball in 1974.

THE OLD HORSEHIDE

A baseball has 108 stitches.

> Baseballs used to be covered with horsehide, but now are covered in cowhide.

The seams of baseballs used in the major leagues are markedly lower than those used in Little League through the college leagues.

HAND IN GLOVE

Baseball players didn't begin to wear a glove until around 1875. Early mitts had no webbing between the thumb and forefinger and were meant more for knocking the ball to the ground than catching it. Webbing didn't appear until 1920, when St. Louis pitcher Bill Doak came up with the idea.

One early wearer of the baseball glove was pitching star Albert Spalding, in 1877. His acceptance of the mitt led other players to wear them.

In 1876, Spalding started the sporting goods business that still bears his name today. Not only did his company sell mitts and baseballs early on, it also designed and made the first volleyball, basketball, and football.

Spalding balls are the official basketball of the National Basketball Association.

HOOPS

In early basketball, a player was disqualified after two fouls. The number was increased to five in 1945.

Before 1901, dribbling was not allowed. The ball could only be bounced one time, after which it could not be shot.

Up until 1938, there was a center jump ball after every score.

The Harlem Globetrotters were actually founded in Chicago in 1926. They are called "Harlem" because of the city's strong black cultural heritage. They didn't play their first game in Harlem until 1968.

THE GRIDIRON

Famed athlete Jim Thorpe helped found the National Football League (known then as the American Professional Football Association) in 1920 and was the league's first president.

Only two of the NFL's original charter teams remain today—the Arizona Cardinals (then the Chicago Cardinals) and the Chicago Bears (then the Decatur Staleys).

The Green Bay Packers are the only nonprofit, community-owned, professional team in the United States.

In 1948, the Los Angeles Rams became the first professional football team to put a logo on their helmets.

BIG BLUE

The New York Giants joined the National Football League in 1925 with an investment of $500 by team owner Tim Mara. A Mara family member, John, is still a co-owner of the team. Bob Tisch bought a 50 percent interest in 1991 (his son Steve now owns his share of the team).

The Giants incorporated as the New York Football Giants to distinguish themselves from the New York Giants baseball team that also played in the city at the same time.

The Giants have the most names/nicknames of any NFL team—New York Football Giants, New York Giants, Giants, G-Men, Big Blue, Big Blue Wrecking Crew, and Jints.

The Giants have no cheerleaders or mascot and don't allow any kind of signs or banners at their stadium.

Jeff Feagles, the Giants current punter, holds the NFL record for most consecutive games played—352 (at the time of this writing). In his career, Feagles has punted the ball the equivalent of forty miles.

NOT SO SUPER BOWL

The first Super Bowl, played on January 15, 1967, was the only Super Bowl that was not a sellout.

Both CBS and NBC simulcast this first game, the only time a Super Bowl has been shown on more than one major network. The NBC broadcast did not finish with their halftime commercials before the second half started and missed the kickoff. The game officials nullified the kickoff and had a re-kick once NBC was ready.

EXTRA POINTS

In the early days of football, the touchdown was worth one point and the point after conversion, known today as the extra point, was worth four points.

Elmo Wright, a receiver for the University of Houston Cougars, performed the first end zone dance in 1969. He later introduced the celebration to the National Football League when he played for the Kansas City Chiefs in 1973.

Before Roger Staubach of the Dallas Cowboys coined the term "Hail Mary," in 1975, a last-second, deep desperation pass was known as a "Big Ben" or an "Alley Oop."

The greatest comeback in NFL history occurred in the 1993 AFC Wildcard Playoff Game between the Houston Oilers and the Buffalo Bills. Frank Reich, the Bills backup quarterback, led them back from a thirty-two-point deficit to a 41–38 overtime win. While in college, Reich had quarterbacked the greatest come-from-behind victory in college football at the time.

Between 1933 and 1977 (with the exception of 1935), the National Football League champions would play a game against a team of college all-stars. The NFL champs had a combined record of 31-9-2 against the all-stars.

There used to be an NFL team in Los Angeles. The Rams played there from 1946 to 1994 The Raiders also played in L.A., from 1982 until 1994.

Before 1981, Stickum and other sticky substances, such as tree sap and glue, were used by NFL receivers and defenders to get a better grip on the ball.

There has never been a shutout in a Super Bowl.

SIS BOOM BAH

Lou Holtz is the only college football coach to lead six different university teams to bowl game appearances— Arkansas, Minnesota, North Carolina, Notre Dame, South Carolina, and William & Mary.

The NCAA Division I Ohio Valley Conference has no schools from the state of Ohio.

The 1942 Rose Bowl was played at Duke University's Wallace Wade Stadium, in Durham, North Carolina, due to fears of a Japanese attack during a West Coast game.

FASTER, HIGHER, STRONGER

The 1900 Paris Olympics and the 1904 St. Louis Olympics were actually a part of the World's Fair being held in each of those cities. The games lasted about five months and included events in mud fighting and greased pole climbing.

General George Patton competed in the 1912 Stockholm Olympics, finishing fifth in the pentathlon.

Dr. Benjamin Spock, author of the classic *Baby and Child Care*, won a gold medal in rowing at the 1924 Paris Olympics.

HOW LOW CAN YOU GO?

The 2000 Paralympics basketball event for the intellectually disabled was won by the Spanish team. They were later stripped of their title, after it was discovered that ten of the twelve players had no disabilities whatsoever.

BLUE BALLS

In 1950, professional tennis and handball player Joe Sobek invented a racket sport that could be played in the thousands of existing YMCA handball courts. He called his new sport, first played at the Greenwich, Connecticut, YMCA "paddle rackets." It later became known as "racquetball."

Hollow rubber balls are used in racquetball, which come in various colors, the most common being blue.

SHUTTLECOCKS

Badminton is named for Badminton House, in Gloucestershire, where the game was introduced to England from India in 1873.

The "birdie" is more appropriately called a shuttlecock. The "shuttle" part comes from it moving back and forth across the net, which resembles the shuttle of a loom. The "cock" part derives from the resemblance to the feathers on a cockerel, or rooster.

A regulation shuttlecock is made of sixteen overlapping goose feathers imbedded in a cork head that is covered with leather.

FAST SERVICE

Bill Tilden was credited with the world's fastest tennis serve, of 163 miles per hour, in 1931. The modern day champ is Andy Roddick, at 155 miles per hour.

PAR FOR THE COURSE

The world's longest golf hole is the par-6, 1,007-yard sixth hole at Chocolay Downs Golf Course in Marquette, Michigan.

The speed of greens on a golf course is measured with a device called a stimpmeter.

Before 1952, when one golfer's ball was positioned in the path of another golfer's ball on the green, the player farthest from the hole had to putt around or over the obstructing ball. This was known as a "stymie."

VERY SUPERSTITIOUS

As a superstition, Wade Boggs drew a symbol meaning "To Life" in the dirt with his bat before every plate appearance.

Michael Jordan wore his college team basketball shorts under his Chicago Bulls shorts, for luck. (As if he needed it.)

Pitcher Turk Wendell had a ritual of eating licorice and brushing his teeth between each inning.

BLIMEY!

The English soccer team Manchester United has been ranked by *Forbes* magazine as the most valuable team in sports, with a worth of $1.87 billion. The Dallas Cowboys are second, at $1.65 billion.

SNEAK ATTACK

Puma and Adidas used to be the same shoe company, started by German brothers Adolph "Adi" Dassler and Rudolph Dassler, in 1924. The brothers became estranged during World War II and Rudolph formed Puma, Adi formed Adidas.

> The brothers' big break came during the 1936 Olympics, when they convinced Jesse Owens to wear a pair of their new spiked running shoes. He won four gold medals, and the orders came pouring in.

The brothers' shoe factory made Panzerschreck anti-tank weapons during World War II.

GIDDY UP

The Belmont Stakes is the oldest of the Triple Crown races, having been first run in 1867.

The Belmont Stakes was canceled in 1911 and 1912, because of New York State's anti-gambling laws.

The Preakness Stakes, held at Pimlico in Baltimore, Maryland, began in 1873, three years before the Kentucky Derby. The race gets its name from the first colt to win a race at Pimlico—Preakness—from Preakness Stables in the Preakness section of Wayne, New Jersey.

From 1894 through 1909, the Preakness was run in Coney Island, New York.

In 1917 and 1922, the Preakness and the Kentucky Derby were run on the same day.

Churchill Downs, where the Kentucky Derby is run, is named after the men who donated the land for the racetrack—John and Henry Churchill.

Triple Crown winner Secretariat still holds the fastest winning time at the Derby, set in 1973. Secratariat also set the Belmont Stakes track record in the same year.

The winner of the Derby receives a blanket of roses; the Preakness winner, a blanket of black-eyed Susans; and the Belmont winner, a blanket of carnations.

Man o' War is considered by many experts as the greatest Thoroughbred of all time. In the post–World War I era, he won twenty out of twenty-one races, his only loss coming to a horse named Upset. This loss is credited with popularizing the word "upset" in describing an underdog beating the favorite.

The term "walkover" comes from British horse racing, where an unopposed horse must walk the course to officially be declared the winner. The comparable American term is "shoo-in."

Quarter horses are so named because of their speed in the quarter mile.

PIKACHU

Pokémon Trading Cards hit the United States in 1998 and became one of the biggest-selling card games in history.

The Pokémon concept came from creator Satoshi Tajiri-Oniwa's fascination with insect collecting. There are 493 Pokémon "species" that players can collect.

FOAMY FUN

NERF stands for "non-expanding recreational foam." The word now has become Internet slang for "weaken."

American inventor Reyn Guyer invented the NERF ball and Twister.

MARIO AND ZELDA

The *Legend of Zelda* and *Super Mario Bros.* video game series were both developed by the same man—Shigeru Miyamoto.

Miyamoto drew his inspiration for *Zelda* from his boyhood experiences wandering around and exploring the countryside around Kyoto.

Guinness World Records Gamer's Edition 2008 named the *Legend of Zelda* series the Highest Rated Game of All Time.

Nintendo was founded in 1889 as a manufacturer of Japanese playing cards. In the 1960s, they became a taxi company and ran a short-stay hotel chain, where lovers could rendezvous. Today, they are the third-richest company in Japan.

THE CUBIST

Erik Akkersdijk of the Netherlands solved the 3×3×3 Rubik's Cube in 7.08 seconds in a 2008 competition.

DISCOVERY ZONE

MOJO

When men get married, their testosterone levels go down. A man's testosterone level also drops by about one-third soon after becoming a father.

Men's testosterone levels go up after a divorce. In fact, research shows that their testosterone levels start to increase one year *before* they get divorced.

Scientists studying testosterone at Yale University have trained chimps to urinate on command so that they can collect samples in cups.

THE BIG O

Studies have revealed that parts of a woman's brain turn off when she has an orgasm, specifically the area responsible for fear and anxiety. Men's orgasms were also studied, but enough data wasn't available because the men climaxed too quickly.

New research indicates that having sex every day improves the genetic quality of a man's sperm and increases his chances of fathering a child. Having sex less frequently will boost sperm count, but reduce fertility, because the sperm are older and less fit.

A man's sperm count is the highest in the afternoon.

JAW BREAKERS

The maxillary and mandibular third molars are more commonly known as wisdom teeth. They are called "wisdom" teeth because they generally come in between the ages of seventeen and twenty-five, when some young adults are thought to gain wisdom.

While most people get four wisdom teeth, it is possible to get more or less.

Fifteen percent of the population never grows any wisdom teeth.

All other toothed mammals, besides humans, have enough room in their jaws for their wisdom teeth. Due to man's changing diet over the millennia, the jaw has shrunk in size, making for a tight fit in many, which is why most people have theirs removed.

Scientists can now harvest stem cells from extracted wisdom teeth.

USELESS ORGANS?

Yes, humans can live without a spleen, but it is not a useless organ. Aside from removing old red blood cells and recycling iron, scientists have recently found that it is a storehouse of immune cells called monocytes—a type of white blood cell.

Likewise, the poor, maligned appendix is not without its virtues. It is a repository of beneficial bacteria that help the digestive system. After a severe bout of diarrhea, these bacteria repopulate the intestines.

VERY GALLING

Another nonessential organ is the gallbladder. It concentrates bile produced in the liver, which it releases to emulsify fatty foods when they enter the digestive tract.

Most vertebrates have gallbladders, the exceptions being horses, deer, llamas, and rats.

Gallstones can range in size from that of a grain of sand up to the size of a golf ball. They are mainly made up of bile components, such as cholesterol, bilirubin, and calcium salts.

Gallstones collected at slaughterhouses and from dogs are an expensive folk remedy used in China.

Solid human waste gets its brown coloration from bile.

THE SKINNY

The average adult has about six pounds of skin.

Rubbing your skin after you bump into something helps to ease the pain, because the signals sent to the brain from doing so interfere with the pain signals.

GRAY ANATOMY

The brain is tannish gray on the outside and yellowish white on the inside, with a soft consistency, like that of tofu.

The brain runs on about twenty watts of power, barely enough to power a very dim lightbulb.

MYSTERIES OF THE MIND

Capgras syndrome is a condition where sufferers are convinced that their family members and friends have been replaced by identical imposters. (Can you say *Twilight Zone*?)

A rare psychiatric disorder, known as a fugue state, involves seemingly normal people forgetting who they are and wandering off to start a new identity. This state can last from hours to months, but is always reversible, with the sufferer regaining full recall of their identity but experiencing amnesia regarding the time that they were in the fugue.

A condition called hemispatial neglect can occur as the result of a brain injury to the right cerebral hemisphere, causing stroke victims to ignore the left half of their visual field. Bizarrely, victims may not be able to see anything on their left side, may only eat the food on the left side of their plate, and only shave or apply makeup to one half of their face.

Foreign accent syndrome is a very rare neurological condition where people begin to speak in a new accent. It generally occurs after a brain injury or stroke.

In rare cases, some people have become suddenly musically gifted after being struck by lightning.

People who work in the creative arts are ten to twenty times more likely to be bipolar, eight to ten times more likely to be depressed, and eighteen times more likely to commit suicide than the general population.

Roughly 15 percent of Americans are dyslexic to one degree or another.

Dyslexia is less commonly noticed in Italy than the United States. This may be because Italian words are spelled more like the way they sound, and therefore reading takes much less effort.

Females don't seem to have panic attacks before they reach puberty.

Multiple sclerosis (MS) gets its name from the fact that the brains of those afflicted have numerous areas of hardened scar tissue. *Sclerosis* is Latin for "scar." The incidence rate of multiple sclerosis increases closer to Earth's poles. It's higher in Minnesota than in Florida.

Most people have few memories before the age of three, because the brain circuitry involved in storing memories doesn't develop until then.

Babies born in the winter and the spring are more prone to schizophrenia.

Males are four times more likely to be autistic than females.

Research done at the University of Virginia indicates that humans' mental abilities peak at age twenty-two and begin a steady decline after twenty-seven.

The Rorschach inkblot test was developed by Swiss psychologist Hermann Rorschach, in 1921. Although he died the following year, his psychology test became popular and is still widely used today.

FORGET-ME-NOT

Alzheimer's disease is named for Alois Alzheimer, a German psychiatrist who first described the condition in 1906.

Women with Alzheimer's live longer than men with Alzheimer's.

People with Alzheimer's have a diminished sense of smell.

COLOR MY WORLD

Synesthesia is a phenomenon wherein people "see" colors associated with different letters or numbers. This neurological mixing of senses can also result in "seeing" colors for musical notes, among many other manifestations. Artists and other creative people are more likely to have synesthesia. Some famous synesthetes were David Hockney, Duke Ellington, and Vladimir Nabokov.

BRAIN SALAD SURGERY

Portuguese doctor António Egas Moniz won the 1949 Nobel Prize for Medicine for pioneering the prefrontal lobotomy.

In 1936, Dr. Walter Freeman performed the first lobotomy in the United States. By 1945, Freeman had "perfected" his technique, which involved inserting an ice pick through the back of the eye sockets and tapping it with a hammer to break through the skull. By moving it side to side, he shredded the nerve connections from the frontal lobe to the thalamus. Freeman toured the country in his "lobotomobile," demonstrating his procedure at mental institutions.

Forty thousand mental patients were lobotomized in the United States, between 1936 and the mid-1960s.

John F. Kennedy's twenty-three-year-old sister, Rosemary, was lobotomized because her father disapproved of her "moodiness." She became mentally incapacitated afterward.

Tennessee Williams' sister, Rose, who had a lobotomy, was the inspiration for the character Laura in his play *The Glass Menagerie*.

FOLLOW YOUR NOSE

After becoming acclimated to a smell, a person doesn't notice it as much. This is because after all the olfactory cells have been stimulated by a specific smell, they stop sending signals to the brain.

Each nostril is tuned to smell certain odors better than others, and this specialization moves back and forth during the day, as the amount of air flowing through each nostril varies over time.

Research has found that smells are more pleasant when sniffed through the right nostril, but the left nostril is better at identifying different odors.

Scientists say humans can remember fifty thousand different scents.

TONGUE 'N' CHEEK

Everyone has a unique tongue print.

Some people have "cloverleaf" tongue, which is the ability to create multiple folds on the edge of the tongue.

The cheeks are known as *buccae* in Latin.

BODY OF KNOWLEDGE

Erector pili muscles are tiny fibers at the base of hair follicles that contract when cold and cause goose bumps.

Adenoids are a type of tonsil in the back of the throat that are often removed with the tonsils. They are there to trap bacteria.

The plica semilunaris is that little red lump of tissue in the corner of the eye. It is all that remains of a third eyelid humans used to have, similar to the nictitating membrane still found in chickens, lizards, and sharks. Its only purpose now is to secrete eye crud, or sleepers.

The ulnar nerve, or funny bone, is the largest unprotected nerve in the body.

There are between 40 and 50 billion fat cells in the human body.

A recent Danish study found that people with thin thighs die sooner than those with larger ones.

There are six muscles in the ear.

Uterus didelphys is a rare condition where a woman has two uteri. There have been cases of women becoming pregnant in both wombs and delivering twins.

People grow a new stomach lining every three or four days. If they didn't, the stomach's acids would dissolve it away.

The big toe, in medical parlance, is called the hallux.

The small intestine is longer than the large intestine, but gets its name because it is smaller in diameter.

A loud snore can reach eighty decibels, the equivalent of a pneumatic drill breaking up concrete. Eighty-five decibels is regarded as dangerous to ear health.

Redheads are more sensitive to pain and need higher doses of anesthetics to numb them than do brunettes and blonds. As a consequence, redheads are twice as likely to avoid going to the dentist.

Women are two and a half times more likely than men to have a ring finger that is longer than the index finger.

The little finger is known as the "pinkie" after the Dutch *pinkje*, meaning "little finger."

BLOODY INTERESTING

The first successful blood transfusion was performed in 1818, but it wasn't until 1901 that ABO blood groups were discovered, making the procedure much safer. The Rh blood group system was found in 1940.

The first blood banks were set up in the Soviet Union in the mid-1930s.

Salt added to blood will keep it from clotting until it is ready to be transfused to a patient.

Sugar added to blood will greatly increase its storage time.

Seven percent of the average person's body weight is blood.

One hundred percent of Chinese people have Rh+ blood.

Cats have four blood types, cows more than eight hundred.

There are about sixty thousand miles of blood vessels in the human body and the heart pumps about two thousand gallons of blood a day.

THE EYES HAVE IT

Visual images are projected unto the retina upside down. The brain flips them upright.

The eye has 120 million rods, which in low light levels see in black-and-white.

The eye has 6 million cones, which see in color and require brighter light to see.

Embryos develop eyelashes in the seventh and eighth weeks.

Eyelashes last about 150 days.

A plucked eyelash requires about two months to grow back.

The Hadza women of Tanzania pluck out all their eyelashes.

In early 2009, the FDA approved the first product to promote eyelash growth—Latisse.

Haemolacria is a rare condition where those afflicted literally cry blood.

WHAT A DRAG

Smoking reduces adult life expectancy by fourteen years.

Smoking kills more Americans each year than AIDS, alcohol, auto accidents, homicide, suicide, and illegal drugs combined.

LE PEW!

Famed anthropologist Louis Leakey believes body odor may have saved early humans from predators, by driving them away.

The Egyptians pioneered the use of deodorants, applying to the armpits cinnamon and other scents that would not go rancid.

Antiperspirants are officially classified as a drug by the Food and Drug Administration, because they alter and/or affect the body's natural functions.

EverDry was the first commercially available antiperspirant, in 1903. It was so acidic that it ate through clothing.

It's the aluminum chlorohydrate in antiperspirants that stains clothes, not sweat.

In San Luis Obispo County, California, libraries, having offensive body odor is illegal.

Matthew McConaughey confessed in 2008 that he does not wear deodorant or antiperspirant. (This may not have been such a revelation to his costars.)

A sixteen-year-old English boy died in 1998 after using too much deodorant. The boy, who was obsessed with hygiene, used to spray his entire body twice a day. Prolonged exposure to the propane and butane in the deodorant proved to be fatally toxic.

SUPER-SIZE IT!

The Journal of Consumer Research reports that, counterintuitively, healthful choice options on a menu actually make people *more* likely to order "unhealthful" foods.

A recent study, published in the *American Journal of Clinical Nutrition*, reveals that organic foods are nutritionally almost identical to ordinary foods.

MOTHER'S LITTLE HELPERS

$228.5 billion worth of name brand drugs were sold in the United States in 2008.

It takes ten to fifteen years and $1.3 billion to develop a new drug.

The average American had 12.5 drug prescriptions filled in 2007.

One in ten American women take antidepressants. One in twenty men do.

Maggots can help heal wounds. Scientists are developing a gel containing enzymes from maggots that can be used to remove decaying tissue from wounds and promote healing.

Between 25 and 50 percent of all prescription drugs in the United States come from plants or were inspired by biochemical models found in plants.

There was a fivefold increase in the use of Ritalin between 1990 and 2000. The United States accounts for 90 percent of the world's Ritalin use.

NOT TONIGHT, DEAR

While women are more likely to use a headache as an excuse to get out of having sex, men are more apt to get a headache *from* having sex.

Cephalgia is the scientific term for "headache."

Accountants get the most headaches of any profession, followed by librarians, construction workers, and bus drivers.

Acetaminophen was first used to treat pain in 1894.

Acetaminophen is the leading cause of liver failure in the United States, sending fifty-six thousand people to the emergency room each year, more than any other drug.

In the fall of 1982, seven people in the Chicago area died after taking Tylenol capsules that had been laced with cyanide. Sales of Tylenol plummeted. The company then introduced the tamper-resistant packaging, enrobed gelcaps, and caplets that are industry standards today.

TRIPPIN'

In 1943, Swiss chemist Albert Hofmann accidentally absorbed through his fingertips some lysergic acid diethylamide, a compound he derived from ergot, a fungus that grows on rye. The chemical is better known as LSD. Hofmann enjoyed the "experience" so much that he ingested the stuff hundreds of times afterward.

Beginning in the 1950s, the Central Intelligence Agency began testing the effects of LSD on their agents, military personnel, prostitutes, the mentally ill, and average citizens, usually without their knowledge or consent.

LSD was outlawed in the United States in 1966.

WE ARE NOT ALONE

There is a wide range of estimates of the actual number of species on Earth, but a general consensus among scientists is around 10 million.

In 2007, 18,516 new species were discovered; half of them were insects.

🌰 UNSEEN WORLD

Approximately one thousand different species of bacteria live on the surface of the skin.

Human saliva contains six hundred different bacteria

In total, some 70 trillion bacterial cells live in and on the body.

Of the estimated 30 million bacteria species, only about seventy are known to cause disease.

The microbe *Pyrolobus fumarii*, which lives on deep sea hydrothermal vents can reproduce at temperatures as high as 235°F.

Most of the medically significant antibiotics come from bacteria that live in soil.

There are about one thousand different kinds of bacteria in a gram of dirt.

Bacteria that were still capable of reproduction have been retrieved from two miles beneath glaciers in Greenland.

I'M RADIOACTIVE

With the discovery of radium, in 1899, several products were marketed to a public fascinated with the element's supposed therapeutic properties. A few follow:

Tho-Radia was a beauty cream sold in France during the early 1930s that contained thorium and radium, both radioactive. It was believed radioactivity killed germs and promoted a healthy glow of the skin.

The Scrotal Radiendocrinator was a product intended to increase sexual virility in men. The device consisted of radium-soaked pieces of paper that were to be placed under the scrotum at night. Its inventor, William J. Bailey, died of bladder cancer in 1949.

Vita Radium Suppositories were sold in the United States to help revitalize "weakened organs."

Revigator was a drinking water laced with radium 266 and 228 isotopes, sold between 1918 and 1928. It was said to cure stomach cancer, among other things. It remained popular in the United States, until well-known industrialist Eben Byers died of jaw cancer after drinking a bottle of the stuff every day for four years.

Radium Chocolate, marketed for its powers of rejuvenation, was sold in Germany from 1931 to 1936.

Doramad radioactive toothpaste was sold in Germany during World War II to kill germs and whiten teeth.

MAKING WAVES

There is no such thing as "the" speed of sound. Sound waves travel at different speeds through air, depending on altitude and temperature, which affect the density of the air. At sea level, in dry air, at 68°F, sound travels at 768 miles per hour. This is about one mile in five seconds.

The speed of sound is 4.4 times faster through water, and fifteen times faster through steel, than through air at sea level, in dry air, at 68°F.

GERONIMO!

A man named Grant Morton is credited with being the first person to parachute from a moving airplane, in 1911, over Venice Beach, California.

More is known about Captain Albert Berry's 1912 jump. The parachute was held in a metal container attached to the bottom of the plane. Berry's weight pulled the parachute free and he floated to earth sitting on a trapeze bar attached to the chute.

BAD BUGS

The bubonic plague is believed to have originated in the Gobi Desert and spread to Byzantium by the sixth century.

During the Second Sino-Japanese War, in 1940–41, the Imperial Army Air Service dropped bombs containing infected fleas on Chinese cities, causing epidemic outbreaks of the plague.

Ten to fifteen people a year contract bubonic plague in the United States.

Each year, between 5 to 20 percent of Americans get the flu. Of those that do, some thirty-six thousand die as a result.

EASY ON THE STARCH

Dry cleaning was discovered by accident, in 1855, when Frenchman John Baptiste Jolly noticed that his tablecloth was clean where his maid had spilled kerosene on it. He later opened the first dry cleaning business.

Early dry cleaners used gasoline and kerosene, then later carbon tetrachloride and trichlorethylene. Today, perchlorethylene is utilized.

BLACK BOXES

Airline flight recorders, also known as black boxes, are not black, but bright orange. They must be able to withstand temperatures of 1000°C.

The installation of black boxes on commercial airliners was prompted by the 1956 midair collision of a TWA jet with a United Airlines jet over the Grand Canyon, which killed 128 people, making it the worst airline disaster of the time.

A SHOCKING DEVELOPMENT

The Taser was developed by a NASA scientist—Jack Cover—between 1969 and 1974.

The word "Taser" is an acronym for Thomas A. Smith's Electric Rifle, a fictional weapon from Victor Appleton's 1911 children's science fiction novel,

Tom Swift and His Electric Rifle. Cover was an avid fan of this book series.

The Taser that failed to subdue Rodney King, in 1991, was ineffective due to a faulty battery.

Law enforcement Tasers have a range of up to thirty-five feet.

Tasers can be legally carried by the public, without a permit, in forty-three states. They are illegal in Hawaii, Massachusetts, Michigan, New Jersey, New York, Rhode Island, Wisconsin, and the District of Columbia.

Pink and leopard-print Tasers are now commercially available. Sales target the female weapons-buying public.

GREEN FLASH, BLUE FLASH

A green flash is a phenomenon where a very quick flash of green light can be seen just after the sun has set, or just before it rises. The flash, which only lasts a second or two, is best seen with an unobstructed horizon, such as over the ocean. It is caused by refraction of the sun's light moving through the lower, denser air along the horizon. On very rare occasions, a blue flash is produced.

STAR POWER

Every second, 4 million tons of mass disappears from the sun, converted into energy.

The Diamond synchrotron particle accelerator in Oxfordshire, England, produces a highly focused beam of light that is 10 billion times brighter than the sun.

The sun is four hundred times bigger than the moon and four hundred times farther from Earth, so the two appear to be the same size in the sky. Because of this perfect symmetry, solar eclipses are possible.

Christopher Columbus was saved from hostilities with the indigenous people of Jamaica by convincing them he was a god. He "predicted" the lunar eclipse of February 29, 1504, that he had read about in his almanac.

Pulsars are stars that can rotate at over six hundred times per second.

OUT OF THIS WORLD

Each year the moon's orbit moves one and a half inches farther away from Earth.

Astronauts who walked on the moon reported suffering irritated eyes, sinuses, and skin from the lunar dust they walked in.

There is a mountain seventeen miles high on Mars.

Because of the tremendous greenhouse effect created by all the carbon dioxide in the atmosphere of Venus, it is the hottest planet, even though Mercury is much closer to the sun.

There are currently 898 satellites orbiting the Earth. The United States owns 463 of them; Russia, 90; and China, 48.

Satellites in geostationary orbit (an orbit in a fixed position above a specific spot on Earth) will take more than one million years to fall to Earth.

There are 300,000 objects between one centimeter and ten centimeters orbiting Earth. There are billions of smaller objects doing so.

🐿 EYE IN THE SKY

The Hubble Space Telescope is named for American astronomer Edwin Hubble.

It was supposed to be launched in 1983, but was delayed until 1990. The *Challenger* shuttle disaster helped to postpone the launch.

Prior to launch, the Hubble had to be stored in a clean room, powered up and purged with nitrogen, at a cost of $6 million a month.

Even though the telescope sat in storage for several years, NASA never realized that its precisely ground mirrors were made to the wrong size, making its images distorted. Corrective optics were installed in 1993.

SPACED OUT

Zero gravity makes body fluids move upward, resulting in puffy faces and nasal congestion, not to mention kidney stone formation, muscle atrophy, bone calcium loss, slower bowels, and a shrinking heart.

After five days at zero gravity, the human body loses 30 percent of its muscle strength.

Astronauts in space don't snore.

Astronauts use liquefied salt and pepper on their food.

Potential astronauts for China's new manned space program have to meet superhuman requirements. They can't have bad breath, body odor, any cavities or scars, any history of colds or sore throats, or history of any serious disease in their family for the past three generations, and, oh yeah, their wives must approve.

DIAMONDS *AREN'T* FOREVER

Diamonds can burn. They are pure carbon, so when they do burn, they are converted to carbon dioxide and just vaporize, with no ash left behind. When houses burn down with jewelry inside, the gold settings can be found in a molten puddle; the diamonds will be gone. Cubic zirconia, on the other hand, will come out of a fire unscathed. (Hear that, guys?)

Diamonds are formed at depths of at least ninety-three miles below the surface of the Earth, at temperatures of between 1650°F and 2370°F.

The diamond is not the hardest substance on Earth. A very rare mineral—lonsdaleite—is 58 percent harder. Lonsdaleite is only found in nature at the site of a meteorite impact. Another rare mineral, wurtzite boron nitride, which is formed by intense volcanic eruptions, is 18 percent harder than diamonds.

Rubies and sapphires are both corundum (aluminum oxide).

Rubies are red because they contain chromium.

Sapphires are all corundum stones that are not red. They get their various colors from other trace elements.

Sapphire glass is so hard that it is used for the windows on grocery store bar code scanners, because it won't scratch.

Emerald is composed of the mineral beryl.

Most emeralds are oiled to improve clarity.

In Brazil, an 840-pound emerald was found that is worth an estimated $400 million.

Ruby is the gift for the fortieth wedding anniversary, sapphire for the forty-fifth, and emerald for the fifty-fifth.

ON THE BEACH

Rip currents can occur in any body of water that has breaking waves, even large lakes.

Strong rip currents can pull people out into open water, even if they are only standing in waist deep water.

About one hundred people in the United States drown each year from rip currents.

More than 80 percent of beach lifeguard rescues are a result of rip currents.

Rip currents are stronger at low tide.

STING OPERATION

Dying jellyfish on the beach can still sting. Shaving cream can be applied to the skin to help the pain and the jelly's stinging cells (nematocysts) can be removed with a razor, knife, or credit card.

A paste of baking soda and water can be applied to remove any venom in the skin.

ROUGH SEAS

A rogue wave, also known as a monster or freak wave, is one that appears out of nowhere, in perfectly calm seas, and may reach heights of ninety-eight feet. They were thought to be the stuff of legend as recently as the 1990s, but now scientific proof is mounting that they really do exist.

WIKI WIKI

A "wiki" is a website that uses collaborative software that allows users to create and edit web pages.

Ward Cunningham developed the first wiki and put it on the Internet in 1995. He chose the term "wiki" after riding on the Wiki Wiki Shuttle buses that run between the terminals at the Honolulu International Airport. In Hawaiian, *wiki* means "quick," and *wiki wiki* means "very quick."

WEBMASTERS

Jorn Barger started what he called a "weblog" of his readings in 1997. Peter Merholz broke the word into "we blog" and later just "blog" in 1997. Evan Williams then came up with the word "blogger."

The country with the fastest Internet speed is South Korea, followed by Japan, Sweden, and Holland. The United States ranks twenty-eighth.

The states with the fastest Internet speed, in order, are Delaware, Rhode Island, New Jersey, Massachusetts, and New York.

The states with the slowest Internet speed are Montana, Alaska, Idaho, Wyoming, and Hawaii.

Microsoft Office was introduced in 1989, in Mac OS. A Windows version came out in 1990.

AUTO ZONE

Radar detectors are illegal in all vehicles in Virginia and Washington, DC.

Car mufflers contain tubes with holes that are engineered so that reflected sound waves will interfere with each other and cancel each other out.

Putting sugar in someone's gas tank does not necessarily disable the car. A better way is to pour water into the tank.

In 1947, Theodore P. Hall developed the Convair 118 Flying Car. It was a sedan car with a wing, tail, engine, and propeller mounted on top. It flew successfully on its two first flights, but crashed on the third after taking off without refueling.

ALARMING DATA

Smoke detectors didn't come into use until 1969.

Smoke detectors can be found in 93 percent of American homes.

At any given time, about 30 percent of smoke detectors are nonfunctioning, mainly because of dead or missing batteries.

GET THE LEAD OUT

In the first half of the sixteenth century, the only large deposit of solid graphite ever found was discovered in England.

Scientists used to think graphite was a form of lead, which is why we still call the center of a pencil "lead."

It was the Italians who came up with the idea of encasing graphite in wood to make the first pencils.

The wood of choice today for pencils is the California incense cedar.

Before the eraser was invented, pencil was removed with bread crumbs.

The first patent for attaching an eraser to the end of a pencil was issued in 1858.

Each year, more than 14 billion pencils are produced.

Pencils write on paper by leaving tiny graphite flecks,

just thousands of an inch long, sticking to the paper fibers.

LISTEN UP

The Sony Walkman portable cassette player was developed in 1979, when engineer Nobutoshi Kihara created the first one so Sony co-chairman Akio Morita could listen to operas during extended airplane flights.

The MP3 format was developed by the Moving Picture Experts Group (MPEG) in the 1990s. It condenses audio files by discarding imperceptible sounds.

The sales of audio CDs have plummeted from $13 billion in 2000, to $5 billion in 2009.

Peer-to-peer shared music files outnumber legal music downloads by a factor of ten.

STICKY STUFF

Scotch (cellophane) tape has a primer on the bottom side to help the glue stick to it, and a release agent on the top side so that the glue will not stick to it.

If you unroll Scotch tape in the very dark room, you will see a faint glow of light, due to a process known as triboluminescence, where light is produced from the breaking of chemical bonds that occur when certain materials are pulled apart or ripped.

Duct tape was created for the U.S. military in 1942 as a water-resistant sealing tape for ammunition cases. After World War II, it was used commercially for sealing air ducts.

PAPER OR PLASTIC?

By some estimates, the plastic shopping bag is the most ubiquitous consumer item in the world, with trillions having been produced.

> Big fish often mistake plastic bags floating in the sea for jellyfish and eat them.

Only about 2 percent of plastic shopping bags are recycled each year in the United States.

> Sixty-three pounds of plastic packaging per person end up in landfills every year.

Plastic makes up 16 percent of municipal solid waste in the United States.

> About 37 percent of plastic soda bottles and 28 percent of plastic water and milk bottles get recycled.

It takes 450 years for a plastic bottle in the ocean to degrade completely.

GOOD VIBRATIONS

As early as the first century, doctors were diagnosing women with a condition known as "hysteria." The word derives from the Greek word for "uterus." They thought hysteria was peculiar to women and caused by disturbances in the uterus.

The commonly accepted medical cure for hysteria was the manual manipulation of the clitoris, by a doctor. The invention of the vibrator in the early 1880s dramatically sped up the doctor's task of inducing an orgasm, making both physicians and their patients very happy.

By the early 1900s, women were ordering vibrators from catalogs and "treating" themselves at home. The vibrator became the fifth electric appliance to enter the American home, following the fan, the sewing machine, the toaster, and the teakettle.

The American Psychiatric Association still recognized hysteria as a condition up until 1952.

MAD COWS

The first cows found to have mad cow disease, more formally known as bovine spongiform encephalopathy, were detected in Britain in 1984. The cows most likely became infected from eating feed that had spinal cords and brains of other cows mixed into it.

A similar disease, called kuru, killed many of the Fore people of Papua New Guinea, who had eaten the brains of their dead during bizarre funeral rites in the mid-1900s.

HOW SWEET IT IS

Half of the sugar produced in the United States each year comes from sugar beets.

Splenda (sucralose) was discovered accidentally by researchers who were actually trying to develop an insecticide. One of the scientists, who had been asked to "test" the chemical, thought he had been asked to "taste" it.

The sweetest compound known is called lugduname. It is more than 200,000 times sweeter than table sugar.

Laboratory rats that drank diet sodas consumed more calories overall than those that drank regular soda. (Not a good sign for dieters.)

IT'S A CHEMICAL REACTION

Small pieces of sodium will dance across the surface of water, while larger pieces will explode.

Glow sticks contain hydrogen peroxide, phenol oxalate ester, and a fluorescent dye. When the first two chemicals are combined, they release energy into the dye, causing its electrons to jump to a higher energy level and back down, releasing energy in the form of light.

The common household multipurpose ABC fire extinguisher contains ammonium phosphate powder, which melts at 350°F and smothers the fire.

A new kind of rubber made from fatty acids can be cut in two and will re-bond (heal) as good as new when the cut ends are put back together.

CAN YOU HEAR ME NOW?

It was Thomas Edison who popularized saying "hello" when answering the telephone.

Yes, a cruise ship has an area code too. It's 871, 872, 873, or 874, depending on where in the world the ship is sailing.

Alexander Graham Bell used ears from human cadavers for his experiments in developing hearing aids.

IT'S ONLY ROCK AND ROLL

WHAT A LONG STRANGE TRIP

The Grateful Dead (known as the Warlocks at the time) were the house band for Ken Kesey's Acid Tests of the mid-1960s—psychedelic parties thrown by the *One Flew Over the Cuckoo's Nest* author. LSD was not illegal at the time. It was LSD chemist Owsley Stanley who initially financed the group.

HAMMER TIME

M.C. Hammer, aka Stanley Kirk Burrell, got his start by dancing in the parking lot of the Oakland Coliseum, home of the Athletics baseball team. He caught the eye of team owner Charlie Finley, who made him a batboy. The players called him "Little Hammer," because of his resemblance to "Hammerin'" Hank Aaron. Two A's players—Dwayne Murphy and Mike Davis—put up twenty thousand dollars each to help launch his Bustin' Records.

NAME THAT BAND

The Dixie Chicks took their name from the Little Feat song "Dixie Chicken."

Journey began as the Golden Gate Rhythm Section.

Pearl Jam used to be called Mookie Blaylock, after the basketball player. Their present name is for a psychedelic confection made by Eddie Vedder's half–Native American great-grandmother—Pearl.

Guns N' Roses took their name from two former bands Axl Rose and Izzy Stradlin were in—L.A. Guns and Hollywood Rose.

Jane's Addiction is named for a prostitute friend of band leader Perry Farrell, who introduced him to fellow members David Navarro and Eric Avery.

The Stone Temple Pilots were originally known as Shirley Temple's Pussy.

The Marshall Tucker Band was named after a blind piano tuner who had rented the building the band rehearsed in before they did.

Molly Hatchet is named for a legendary Southern hooker who supposedly castrated and mutilated her clients.

MUSICAL MONIKERS

Early in his career, Billy Joel played in piano bars under the name Bill Martin.

Ringo Starr, born Richard Starkey, got his "Ringo" nickname because he wore so many rings.

Kid Rock's real name is Robert James Ritchie.

Tina Turner was born Anna Mae Bullock.

Marvin Lee Aday is better known as Meatloaf.

Sting picked up his nickname because he used to wear a yellow and black striped shirt.

Calvin Broadus was nicknamed "Snoop" (Doggy Dogg) by his mom.

Cat Stevens was born Steven Demetri. He changed his name to Yusef Islam after becoming a Muslim.

George Michael was born Georgios Kyriacos Panayiotou.

Freddie Mercury was born Farrokh Bulsara, a Parsi from an Indian-based Zoroastrian community.

John Lydon, of the Sex Pistols, was called Johnny Rotten by bandmate Steve Jones, who didn't care for his hygiene.

BAD BOYS

Everclear's frontman, Art Alexakis, was hooked on heroin by age thirteen. His older brother and girlfriend both died of overdoses before he kicked the habit at twenty-two.

AC/DC's vocalist Bon Scott died by choking on his own vomit in 1979.

On the album cover of *The Allman Brothers Band at Fillmore East*, Duane Allman is hiding some cocaine in his lap, which explains why all the members are laughing.

In 1969, a fan was stabbed to death by members of the Hells Angels that were providing security at the Rolling Stones concert at California's Altamont Speedway. Some critics blamed the song "Sympathy for the Devil" for causing the killing, and the Stones refrained playing it again for six years.

Sid Vicious was charged with stabbing his girlfriend Nancy Spungen to death in their Chelsea Hotel room. He died of a heroin overdose before going to trial.

Jim Gordon, the drummer on the Derek and the Dominos song "Layla," is a schizophrenic who killed his mother with a hammer in 1983.

DANGEROUS PROFESSION

While performing at the 1992 Video Music Awards show, Nirvana bassist Chris (now known as Krist) Novoselic threw his guitar up in the air, but forgot to move out of the way. The bass hit him in the head, knocking him silly.

Soul singer Curtis Mayfield was paralyzed from the neck down after stage lighting fell on him at an outdoor concert at Brooklyn's Wingate Field in 1990.

Aerosmith's Steven Tyler fell off a stage in South Dakota, injuring his head, neck, and shoulders, causing the band to suspend their 2009 tour.

THAT'LL BE THE DAY

Charles Hardin "Buddy" Holley became Buddy Holly when Decca Records misspelled his last name on his first contract.

Holly's "That'll Be the Day" gets its name from a line John Wayne says repeatedly in the 1956 movie *The Searchers*.

Holly pioneered the basic two guitars, one bass, and drums rock band setup.

🎵 THE DAY THE MUSIC DIED

On February 3, 1959, Buddy Holly, weary of riding on a bus, chartered a small plane to take him and bandmates Waylon Jennings and Tommy Allsup from Iowa to Minnesota. Jennings gave up his seat to the Big Bopper, who had the flu, and Tommy Allsup lost his seat to Richie

Valens on the flip of a coin. The plane went down a few minutes after takeoff in snowy, windy conditions, killing all aboard.

The crash received little media attention at the time because American Airlines Flight 320 crashed the same day at New York's LaGuardia Airport, killing sixty-five.

GENERATION GAP

In 1962, the Beatles received a rejection letter from the Decca Recording Company saying that they didn't like their sound and guitar music was on the way out.

The Beatles first "appeared" on American television on January 4, 1964, when *The Jack Paar Program* aired a film of them performing "She Loves You." Paar prefaced the clip by saying, "I understand science is working on a cure for this."

HAVE IT YOUR WAY?

The Modern English song "I Melt With You" was used in Burger King commercials during the late 1990s, without the band's consent, even though their keyboardist was a vegan. Unfortunately, they didn't own the rights to the tune.

DITCHED DAY JOBS

Mick Jagger once sold ice cream and worked in a mental hospital.

Ozzy Osbourne worked in a slaughterhouse. (Seems about right.)

Chubby Checker plucked chickens.

Rod Stewart dug graves.

James Brown racked balls in a billiard room.

Gene Simmons of Kiss was a schoolteacher in Manhattan.

Phil Spector once worked as a court stenographer.

Fred Durst of Limp Bizkit used to be a tattoo artist. (No way!)

Korn's vocalist, Jonathan Davis, worked as a mortuary assistant.

Bette Midler used to be a go-go dancer in a New Jersey bar.

Alanis Morissette acted on the Nickelodeon children's show *You Can't Do That on Television* at the age of ten.

Wladziu Valentino Liberace made a living playing piano in Milwaukee cabarets and strip bars during the Great Depression.

DIVAS

Whitney Houston was often hours late for rehearsals, interviews, and photo shoots, and canceled tour dates due to her use of drugs. She has since apparently cleaned up her act.

In 1983, Diana Ross promised to donate $250,000 from two concerts at New York's Central Park to build a new playground. She later claimed the shows didn't make enough money for her to do so. It wasn't until Mayor Ed Koch castigated her for the next five months that she was shamed into paying up.

Mariah Carey was the only artist to have a number one *Billboard* hit in every year of the 1990s.

Jewel grew up in a log cabin on an eight-hundred-acre Alaskan homestead that had no running water. She briefly lived in her VW van after moving to California.

Shania Twain lived in a Toronto homeless shelter with her mother and sisters when she was thirteen.

Bonnie Raitt's father, John Raitt, was a Broadway singer, who starred in *Carousel* and *The Pajama Game*.

Sinéad O'Connor supported herself by delivering singing "kiss-o-grams" in a French maid outfit when she was sixteen. O'Connor was "ordained" by a Roman Catholic offshoot and goes by the name of Mother Bernadette Maria.

Joni Mitchell had polio as a child and spent her time in the children's hospital singing. A down-on her-luck Mitchell put her newborn daughter up for adoption in 1965.

ON THE ROAD AGAIN

Willie Nelson picked cotton as a child. He later sold Bibles and encyclopedias door-to-door.

In 1990, the Internal Revenue Service fined Nelson $16.7 million and seized most of his assets, forcing him to auction off nearly all of his belongings. In 1991, he sold his album *The IRS Tapes: Who'll Buy My Memories?* direct to the public through an 800 number, with the profits going directly to the IRS.

MONKEY BUSINESS

The Monkees were a band created by Columbia Pictures executives, inspired by the Beatles movie *A Hard Day's Night*.

Originally, the producers considered hiring the Dave Clark Five, but decided to go with four unknowns.

Five hundred actors auditioned for the Monkees' TV show. Harry Nilsson, Paul Williams, and Stephen Stills were all rejected, but Stills did recommend his room-mate, Peter Tork, for the show.

None of the four Monkees played the instruments on their first two albums. They only supplied the vocals.

Davy Jones got a draft notice after the first season wrapped, and he fasted for three weeks so he would fail his physical.

FLEA

Red Hot Chili Peppers bass player Flea (Michael Balzary) played Sylvester Stallone's son in the 1976 film *F.I.S.T.* Flea also did the voice for the character "Donny" on Nickelodeon's cartoon series *The Wild Thornberries*.

Flea was given his nickname by the Chili Peppers' singer, Anthony Kiedis, while they were on a skiing trip, because Balzary was so jumpy and unpredictable.

In 1990, Flea and drummer Chad Smith went into the audience during a performance at the *MTV Spring Break* special. Flea threw an unsuspecting girl over his shoulder and Smith proceeded to spank her. Flea and Smith were convicted of battery and Flea of sexual harassment.

NIN

Trent Reznor of Nine Inch Nails is a one-man show. He writes, performs, arranges, and produces all of NIN's songs.

Reznor has a taste for the macabre. He moved into the Los Angeles house where the Manson Family members killed Sharon Tate, to record an album in 1994. When he moved out, Reznor took with him the infamous front door on which the murderers had scrawled the word "PIG" in Tate's blood.

ROCKET MAN

At the age of eleven, Reginald Dwight (Elton John) won a piano scholarship to the prestigious Royal Academy of Music.

John hooked up with songwriter Bernie Taupin after they both responded to the same ad in a music trade publication. Although they had a long and wildly successful musical collaboration, John and Taupin rarely met or discussed their songs. Taupin would write the lyrics at a frenetic pace, sometimes a song an hour, and John would compose music to fit them.

Elton has a collection of outrageous sunglasses that cost him around forty thousand dollars.

Captain Fantastic was the first album to enter the *Billboard* charts at number one.

"Candle in the Wind 1997," Elton's tribute to Princess Diana, became the fastest and biggest selling single of all time.

TONE IT DOWN

Tone-Lōc (born Anthony Terrell Smith) acquired his gravelly voice due to his grandmother giving him scalding hot tea with brandy as a cold remedy.

In 1993, Tone-Lōc smashed the windows of a woman's car with a baseball bat and was sentenced to one hundred hours of community service.

LEFT EYE

Lisa "Left Eye" Lopes, of TLC, got her nickname by wearing a condom taped over the left lens of her glasses early in her career.

In 1994, Lopes burned down the house of her boyfriend, Atlanta Falcons wide receiver Andre Rison, after an argument. In 1995, she had to file for bankruptcy when she couldn't come up with the $1.3 million she owed Lloyds of London for the fire.

B.B.

B.B. King (Riley B. King) picked cotton as a child.

King was a DJ on a Memphis black radio station, where he was known as the "Beale Street Blues Boy." This was later shortened to "B.B."

METAL HEADS

Metallica was the biggest selling rock group of the 1990s.

Since 1991, Metallica is the fourth-highest selling artist worldwide, moving 51 million albums in the United States.

On September 26, 1986, the original Metallica bassist, Cliff Burton, was killed in an accident involving the band's bus, while touring in Sweden. The group members had drawn cards to choose bunks the night before. Burton drew the ace of spades and picked the most comfortable sleeping compartment. Unfortunately, the bus skidded and flipped over numerous times, ejecting Burton and pinning his body beneath the vehicle. The rest of the band emerged unscathed.

The swirling, blobby solution pictured on Metallica's *Load* album cover was a mixture of photographer Andres Serrano's own semen and bovine blood, pressed between two sheets of Plexiglas.

In 1977, Marvel Comics published a Kiss comic book that contained some of the band members' blood in the red ink. It sold 400,000 copies.

THE PELVIS

Elvis has sold over 1 billion records worldwide. He had 149 singles on the *Billboard* charts, including forty top tens and eighteen number ones. Elvis had thirty-four consecutive top ten pop hits. The Beatles had thirty-three.

Elvis adopted his trademark pompadour hairstyle after he graduated from high school and planned on becoming a truck driver. This was the trucker's style at the time. He had dirty blond hair, but dyed it black with a ducktail to copy his favorite actor—Tony Curtis.

In 1954, a teenage Elvis made his only appearance at the Grand Ole Opry. Apparently the crowd didn't care for his rockabilly music, and management asked him never to return. He never did.

Graceland used to be a church, before it was converted into a twenty-three-room mansion.

Presley's agent, Colonel Parker, turned down an offer for Elvis to costar with Barbra Streisand in the remake of *A Star Is Born*, because he refused to give equal billing.

Elvis never performed outside of the United States, except for a few shows in Canada in 1957.

Late in his career, Elvis was so fat that he would rip his pants on stage.

On August 16, 1977, Elvis was found dead, four days after a tell-all book—*Elvis: What Happened?*—was published, detailing his problem with drugs.

The Presley family kept the autopsy results sealed, but his physician—Dr. George Nichopoulus—was charged with prescribing Elvis ten thousand amphetamines, barbiturates, and other narcotics in the seven months before he died.

A photograph of his corpse, taken by a cousin, appeared on the cover of the *National Enquirer*, making it their bestselling issue ever.

BABS

Barbra Streisand began her career singing in Greenwich Village gay bars in the early 1960s. She gave up on performing in public for more than twenty years after a 1967 death threat and developing a severe case of stage fright.

SILLI VANILLI

Fabrice Morvan and Rob Pilatus, the front men for Milli Vanilli, were outed as lip-synching fakes in 1989, when the recording of "Girl You Know It's True" began to skip at a live MTV performance. The pair ran off stage in disgrace. As a result, twenty-seven lawsuits were filed for fraud. A court ruled that anyone who could prove they had purchased the album was entitled to a three-dollar rebate. More than eighty thousand claims were submitted.

STAGE FRIGHT

Rod Stewart had such a bad case of stage fright on the night of his first performance with the Jeff Beck Group that he sang the opening number from backstage at New York's Fillmore East.

Van Morrison also suffered from severe stage fright, once walking off stage in the middle of a show and not returning.

WHAT'S WRONG WITH THIS PICTURE?

Chevy Chase played drums with Bad Rock Group, an early incarnation of Steely Dan.

Steven Tyler was the drummer when Aerosmith formed in 1970.

DUTCH BOYS

Upon moving to America from the Netherlands when they were young, Eddie Van Halen learned to play the drums, while his brother Alex learned guitar. They later traded instruments before forming their first band—Mammoth.

Van Halen was discovered by Kiss front man Gene Simmons while they were playing a club in Los Angeles, and he paid for the band to record a demo tape.

As of 2007, the band had the most number one hits on the *Billboard* mainstream rock chart.

JOHNNY B. GOODE

Chuck Berry was a hairdresser before he made it big.

Berry was imprisoned for two years after he brought a fourteen-year-old Apache girl from Texas across state lines to work in his St. Louis nightclub. He had previously spent three years in reform school for a carjacking incident in 1944.

More recently, Berry served one hundred days in jail for tax evasion in 1979.

In 1990, Berry was charged with marijuana possession and secretly videotaping fifty-nine women, one a minor, using the restrooms at two restaurants he owned. He pleaded down and received a six-month suspended sentence.

TOO GOOD TO BE TRUE?

Paul McCartney wrote "Yesterday" one night after he woke up from a dream with the melody in his head. He thought that he must have heard it somewhere and waited on recording it for fear of plagiarism. After asking all his friends in the music biz if they recognized it, he decided to record the tune.

"Yesterday" holds the record for the song with the most cover versions in history.

Paul's bandmate George Harrison should have followed Paul's example. In 1976, Harrison was found guilty of unconsciously plagiarizing the Chiffons song "He's So Fine" in his hit song "My Sweet Lord." Harrison was so upset about the matter that he wrote "This Song," about the case.

Crytomnesia is inadvertent plagiarism, where people think they have a novel creation but have actually heard or seen it before.

I WRITE THE SONGS

Beach Boy Bruce Johnson wrote the song "I Write the Songs," not Barry Manilow. Barry turned it into a number one hit after David Cassidy and Captain & Tennille had recorded their own versions of the song.

Joni Mitchell wrote the song "Woodstock," although she skipped the concert to appear on *The Dick Cavett Show*. She composed the song while watching coverage of the event on TV in a Manhattan hotel room.

"We've Only Just Begun" was written by Paul Williams and Roger Nichols for a Crocker National Bank (California) commercial in 1970.

The Paul Simon song "Mother and Child Reunion" comes from a chicken and egg dish Simon saw on a restaurant menu in New York's Chinatown.

The Boomtown Rats song "I Don't Like Mondays" was inspired by a January 29, 1979, shooting spree in San Diego that killed two adults and wounded eight children in a school playground. The murderer remarked, "I don't like Mondays. This livens up the day."

The Tallahatchie Bridge, which Billy Joe McAllister jumped off of in the 1967 Bobbie Gentry song "Ode to Billie Joe," was located in Greenwood, Mississippi. It collapsed in 1972.

"Stairway to Heaven," like many of Led Zeppelin's hits, was never released as a single.

The song "Happy Days Are Here Again" was released in October 1929, just before the stock market crashed. The tune did help to cheer people up and was Franklin Delano Roosevelt's theme song for his successful 1932 run for president. It has been a staple at Democratic conventions ever since.

"Chopsticks" (formerly known as "The Celebrated Chop Waltz") was composed by sixteen-year-old Euphemia Allen, in 1877.

SINGING THE BLUES

The singer Meatloaf went bankrupt twice, due to his managers stealing from him.

Mick Fleetwood, of Fleetwood Mac fame, went bust in 1984, after "blowing" $8 million on his cocaine habit.

Isaac Hayes lost it all when his record company would not pay him and he in turn could not pay his bank loans.

Andy Gibb went bankrupt in 1987 and died a drug-related death one year later.

Marvin Gaye was reduced to living in a van in Hawaii in 1979, after a divorce, problems with the IRS, and drugs tapped him out. His father shot him to death after an argument in 1984, with a gun Marvin had bought for him four months prior.

SURFIN' SAFARI

The only Beach Boy who actually surfed was Dennis Wilson, who drowned while boating in 1983.

The Beach Boys were supposed to be called the Pendletones, after the Pendletone woolen shirts that were fashionable at the time. When they recorded their first single—"Surfin'"—a worker at the studio changed the band's name to "Beach Boys" on the record labels to tie in with the surfer movement. The band didn't have enough money to have the labels changed and just stuck with the new name.

Glen Campbell was briefly a Beach Boy, when he filled in for anxiety-ridden Brian Wilson on their 1965 concert tour.

THE GRAMMY GOES TO . . .

The Grammy Awards used to be called the "Gramophone Awards," which is why the statuette depicts an old gramophone.

The first Grammy Awards were given out in 1958.

SOUNDS JUST LIKE
A COUNTRY SONG

Garth Brooks met his first wife, Sandy Mahr, when he was a nightclub bouncer. Mahr was involved in a brawl in the ladies' room. When Brooks rushed in, he found her with her fist stuck in the wall. Although he ejected her from the club, he thought she was very pretty and started to date her.

LED NOBS?

During a 1970 concert in Copenhagen, Denmark, Led Zeppelin had to play under a different name—the Nobs—after the threat of a lawsuit by Eva von Zeppelin, a descendant of Count Ferdinand von Zeppelin, the airship's creator.

BEHIND THE MUSIC

The Eagles were once Linda Ronstadt's backup band.

Enya is the second bestselling Irish artist, after U2.

Thomas Dolby, who had a hit in the 1980s with "Blinded by Science," now writes and records ringtones. And no, he has nothing to do with Dolby Laboratories, of Dolby noise reduction fame.

Paul Anka's first 45 record sold just three hundred copies. His second—"Diana"—has sold over 9 million copies.

Little Richard gave up rock-and-roll music in 1957, after he had a vision of his own damnation. He declared rock to be the devil's music and became a minister in the Seventh-day Adventist Church. He later returned to rock and roll.

Paul Simon and Art Garfunkel started singing together in sixth grade in Forest Hills, New York.

Brian "Dexter" Holland of the Offspring graduated class valedictorian of his high school.

The members of spoof band Spinal Tap all played their own instruments and wrote their own songs.

When Les Paul broke his right elbow in 1948, he had it set in a position that allowed him to still play guitar.

Journey guitarist Neal Schon dropped out of high school at fifteen to play with Santana. He turned down playing with Eric Clapton's Derek and the Dominos, because Santana had called him first. He later left to form the band Journey.

Loretta Lynn was married at thirteen. She had her first child at fourteen and was a grandmother at twenty-nine.

Abba was the most commercially successful band of the 1970s. At one time, they were the second most profitable corporation in Sweden.

Squeeze never had an album in the *Billboard* top thirty, but their greatest hits went platinum.

John Mellencamp suffered from spina bifida as a child.

HOW OLD ARE YOU NOW?

The lyrics to "Happy Birthday to You" were made up by Louisville, Kentucky, kindergarten kids around the turn of the twentieth century.

Time Warner Inc. owns the song today and forbids it to be sung in public without paying a healthy royalty. This is why chain restaurants create their own dopey birthday songs to sing to customers.

CLASSICAL CORNER

After Beethoven went deaf, he could still compose music by biting down on a rod connected to the soundboard of his piano that would transfer the musical vibrations to his jaw and help him better perceive the sound.

Mozart started playing the keyboard at three and composing music at five.

Johann Sebastian Bach fathered twenty children, by two wives; only ten of whom survived into adulthood.

LINER NOTES

Billboard magazine began in Cincinnati in 1896 as *Billboard Advertising* magazine, a trade paper for the bill posting industry. They covered circuses, carnivals, and amusement parks in the early 1900s. It was the advent of the jukebox that got *Billboard* interested in ranking song popularity in the 1930s.

The only vice president of the United States to ever compose a number one hit pop song was Charles Dawes, who served under Calvin Coolidge. In 1911, Dawes composed Melody in A Major. In 1951, Carl Sigman wrote lyrics for the tune—"It's All in the Game"—and it was recorded by several artists. It wasn't until 1958, however, when Tommy Edwards released a rock-and-roll version, that it went to the top of the *Billboard* charts.

Dorothy Rodgers, wife of composer Richard Rodgers, invented the disposable toilet brush on a stick—the Jonny Mop—after becoming frustrated one day while cleaning her john.

The saxophone was invented, in the 1840s, by Belgian instrument maker Adolphe Sax.

At the Movies

"FATHER" OF CINEMA

Hannibal Goodwin, an Episcopal minister from Newark, New Jersey, created the first celluloid roll film in 1887.

WHAT THEY WERE ALMOST CALLED

Many of the most successful movies almost had some pretty lame titles:

Back to the Future—Spaceman from Pluto

Pretty Woman—3,000 (the dollar amount offered to the hooker character for the week)

Help!—Eight Arms to Hold You

Tootsie—Would I Lie to You? (*Tootsie* was suggested by Dustin Hoffman. It was the name of his mother's dog.)

Blazing Saddles—Tex X

Annie Hall—Anhedonia (the scientific term for the inability to experience pleasure)

American Graffiti—Another Slow Night in Modesto (Producer Francis Ford Coppola wasn't crazy about the title and suggested that director George Lucas change the name.)

BERRY INTERESTING

Halle Berry lived in a homeless shelter at the age of twenty-one, after her mother cut her off.

Halle Berry's stunt double in *Catwoman* was a man— martial arts expert Nito Larioza.

Berry was the 1986 Miss USA first runner-up.

She also was the driver in two hit-and-run accidents.

Nicole Kidman was born in Honolulu in 1967 and returned with her parents to Australia when she was four.

Nicolas Cage is the nephew of Francis Ford Coppola. He changed his name from Nicolas Coppola to avoid the appearance of nepotism.

Tom Hanks is the highest grossing actor of all time.

Goldie Hawn is a direct descendant of Edward Rutledge, a signer of the Declaration of Independence.

Sigourney Weaver was born Susan Alexander Weaver. At age fourteen, she began calling herself Sigourney, after Sigourney Howard, a minor character in the F. Scott Fitzgerald novel *The Great Gatsby*.

Whoopi Goldberg was christened Caryn Elaine Johnson. Early in her career, she went by the name "Whoopi Cushion," a nickname she picked up for being overly gassy. She later dropped the "Cushion" and added "Goldberg," after some Jewish relatives.

River Phoenix had four siblings—Rain, Summer, Liberty, and Joaquin (previously known as Leaf).

During the filming of *The Adventures of Marco Polo* in 1938, Lana Turner had her eyebrows shaved off. They never grew back.

Harrison Ford became a carpenter when his first attempt at acting failed. Ford acquired the scar on his chin when he tried to buckle his seat belt while driving and had an accident.

Jack Lemmon was born in a hospital elevator. Lemmon's first role was in an army training film that warned against the dangers of loose women and venereal disease.

CRUISE CONTROL

Tom Cruise's family moved around a lot. He attended fifteen schools by the time he was fourteen.

Cruise decided to go into acting after winning the lead in his high school's production of *Guys and Dolls*.

He writes with his right hand, but does most other things with his left.

Cruise was introduced to Scientology by his first wife, Mimi Rogers.

YO, ADRIAN

Sylvester Stallone attended beauty school after graduating high school.

His first lead role was in the 1970 soft-core porn movie *Party at Kitty and Stud's*.

Stallone has five children—Sage Moonblood, Seargeoh, Sophia Rose, Sistine Rose, and Scarlet Rose.

CHAIRMAN OF THE BOARD

Frank Sinatra's mother was convicted twice for running an illegal abortion clinic out of their Hoboken, New Jersey, home.

Sinatra was delivered by forceps, which punctured his eardrum and left a scar on his cheek. His parents were hoping for a girl and had already picked out the name Frances.

Frank was expelled from high school, after completing just forty-seven days.

In 1968, he divorced his third wife, Mia Farrow, after she refused to stop filming *Rosemary's Baby* and do a movie with him.

According to Mia Farrow, Frank offered to have Woody Allen's legs broken when Allen started dating Farrow's adopted daughter Soon-Yi.

Frank was banned from Marilyn Monroe's funeral by Joe DiMaggio.

Frank Sinatra's son, Frank Sinatra Jr., was kidnapped at Harrah's Lake Tahoe in 1963. Frank paid a ransom of $240,000. The kidnappers demanded that Frank communicate with them by pay phone, so he kept a roll of dimes in his pocket during the ordeal, a practice he continued for the rest of his life.

There was a clause in Sinatra's will that anyone who contested it would be disinherited.

GRACE, DIGNITY, AND TALENT

Prince Rainier of Monaco demanded and received a $2 million dowry when he married Grace Kelly.

She broke off her engagement to fashion designer Oleg Cassini to marry Rainier.

The accident that killed Kelly was believed to have resulted from her suffering a stroke while driving.

She "graced" the cover of the first issue of *USA Today* in 1982.

Someone from Monaco is called a Monegasque.

THE LATIN LOVER

Rudolph Valentino was born Rodolfo Alfonso Raffaello Piero Filiberto Guglielmi.

Actress Jean Acker locked him out of their hotel room on their wedding night. The marriage never was consummated.

He died at the age of thirty-one, in such debt that there was no money to bury him.

One hundred thousand mourners lined up outside the New York City funeral home that held his viewing. Riots broke out in the line and despondent women were said to have committed suicide.

DON'T QUIT YOUR DAY JOB

Warren Beatty used to catch rats and other rodents before he made it big.

Amy Adams was a Hooters girl.

Matthew McConaughey shoveled chicken manure.

One Flew Over the Cuckoo's Nest author Ken Kesey once worked as an orderly in a mental institution, where he took LSD for "research" purposes.

Danny DeVito was a beauty therapist in his sister's hair salon.

Whoopi Goldberg used to lay bricks.

Johnny Depp parlayed his career as a pen salesman into stardom.

DOWN AND OUT *BEFORE* BEVERLY HILLS

At one point in his life, Daniel Craig slept on park benches in London.

When Jim Carrey was young, he lived in a van with his family.

Hilary Swank and her mom lived in a car when they moved to Los Angeles.

SANDY!

Grease was released in Spain as *Brilliantina*, because its English name translated as "fat" in Spanish.

Most of the cast in this teen musical were in their mid to late twenties. Olivia Newton-John was twenty-nine and Stockard Channing was thirty-four.

Henry Winkler, who played Fonzie on *Happy Days*, was asked to play Danny Zuko, but he turned it down for fear of becoming typecast.

Jeff Conaway had to slouch whenever being filmed with John Travolta, to make Travolta look taller.

Conaway's character—Kenickie—was supposed to sing "Greased Lightning," but Travolta pressured the producers to let him do it.

Conaway gave Channing real hickeys for her Rizzo character to sport.

MAKE MY DAY

Frank Sinatra was almost cast as Harry Callahan in the movie *Dirty Harry*. He decided against the role because the big gun he would have had to wield aggravated an earlier wrist injury. Steve McQueen and Paul Newman were approached next, but declined. It was Newman, however, who suggested Clint Eastwood for the part.

The part of Callahan was loosely based on real life detective David Toschi, who was the chief investigator in the Zodiac killer case.

The film was originally titled *Dead Right*.

The name "Clint Eastwood" is an anagram for "old west action."

When directing, Eastwood says "okay," instead of "action" and "cut."

Clint Eastwood and Burt Reynolds were both fired early in their careers by the same director. Clint was canned because his Adam's apple was too big and Burt for shoving the director into a pool of water.

PHONE HOME

A two-foot, two-inch actor played E.T. in the 1981 film, except in the kitchen scenes, where a ten-year-old boy who was born with no legs filled in.

The face of E.T. is a composite of Albert Einstein, Carl Sandburg, and a pug dog.

AN OFFER HE CAN'T REFUSE

In *The Godfather*, a fake horse head was used for rehearsals of the famous scene, but a real one, obtained from a dog food plant, was used in the final shot. The scream by actor John Marley was genuine, since he didn't know ahead of time about the real head.

Marlon Brando read most of his lines from cue cards.

Francis Ford Coppola used many of his relatives as extras in the movie.

I'M THE KING OF THE WORLD!

Titanic was the first movie to have a $200 million budget. This is more than the actual ship would cost to build today.

If the studio had had its way, Matthew McConaughey would have been cast as Jack, instead of Leonardo DiCaprio, who was director James Cameron's pick. Macaulay Culkin was also considered for the role.

On the final night of filming in Nova Scotia, some miscreant laced the cast and crew's clam chowder with angel dust, causing eighty of them to become ill and hallucinate.

Kate Winslet came down with pneumonia when shooting the water scenes after she refused to wear a wet suit.

YOU'RE GONNA NEED A BIGGER BOAT

The mechanical shark in the movie *Jaws* was nicknamed "Bruce," after director Steven Spielberg's lawyer. He often referred to it as the "great white turd" because it malfunctioned so frequently.

The mechanical shark was never tested in the water, and when they put it in the sea off Martha's Vineyard to begin filming, it immediately sank to the bottom.

During preproduction, George Lucas stuck his head inside the mechanical shark to see how it worked. As a prank, Steven Spielberg used the controls to close the mouth and Lucas's head became stuck in the beast.

Spielberg's real life dog played Police Chief Brody's dog.

Robert Shaw, who played Quint, could not stand Richard Dreyfuss, who played Hooper.

Shaw was in trouble with the IRS at the time and fled the country as soon as filming was completed.

MAY THE FORCE BE WITH YOU

In the movie *Star Wars*, Carrie Fisher's breasts were taped down, since underwear wouldn't have looked right beneath her flowing white outfit.

Originally, the studio felt that Chewbacca should wear some type of clothing.

Chewbacca's voice was created using the sounds of badgers, bears, camels, and walruses.

The sound of the TIE fighters was created by combining a young elephant squealing with the noise of a car passing by on a wet road.

Mark Hamill ruptured a blood vessel in his face from holding his breath so long while underwater in the trash compactor scene.

The word "Jedi" comes from the Japanese samurai soap opera genre—*Jidai Geki*.

David Prowse, who played Darth Vader, claimed that he was unaware that his voice had been dubbed over with that of James Earl Jones's until he saw the movie on opening night.

Frank Oz, who did the voices of Miss Piggy, Fozzie the Bear, and Cookie Monster, was the voice of Yoda.

WHAT'S UP, DOC?

According to his creators, Bugs Bunny was "born" in Brooklyn in 1940 and has a Flatbush accent, with a little Bronx dialect mixed in.

Bugs became the first cartoon character to be pictured on a U.S. postage stamp. His stamp is the seventh most popular with collectors.

Bugs's trademark of chewing a carrot while casually leaning up against a tree was taken from a similar scene in the 1934 hit comedy movie, *It Happened One Night*, where Clark Gable munched on a carrot.

Bugs wears white gloves. The only time he ever removed one was in the 1949 cartoon short—*Long-Haired Hare*—when he conducts an orchestra.

In 2002, *TV Guide* voted Bugs the greatest cartoon character of all time.

Skunk Pepé Le Pew won an Oscar for the 1949 Best Short Subject (Cartoon)—*For Scent-imental Reasons.*

Pluto was called Rover in his first animated short, in 1930, and from then on was known as Pluto the Pup.

SINGIN' IN THE RAIN

In the 1952 film *Singin' in the Rain*, Gene Kelly had a fever of 103 the day they shot his famous dance number in the rain. Kelly ad-libbed most of the scene, which he did in one take.

The rain for this famous scene consisted of a water-milk mixture, which showed up better on film than plain water. The milk in the rain caused Kelly's wool suit to shrink.

Production had to be halted for several hours after it was discovered that Cyd Charisse's pubic hair could be seen through her costume.

SHAKEN, NOT STIRRED

Roger Moore was forty-five when he started playing James Bond, in *Live and Let Die*. He was fifty-seven in *A View to a Kill*.

Dr. No, the first James Bond movie, was released in Japan as *We Have No Need of a Doctor*.

Sean Connery started balding as a young man and wore a toupee in all of his Bond movies.

THAT'LL DO, PIG

In the 1995 movie *Babe*, forty-eight Yorkshire piglets were used for the title role. Pigs grow so fast, this many were needed to maintain continuity over the five-month filming schedule. An animatronic pig was also employed.

Makeup artists applied eyelashes and a hairpiece to each Babe.

Over one thousand animals were used and fifty-six animal trainers were on the set.

The actor who played Babe's owner—James Cromwell—only spoke 171 words in the entire movie.

MY PRECIOUS

J.R.R. Tolkien sold the movie rights to *The Lord of the Rings* in 1968, for $15,000.

The entire *The Lord of the Rings* film trilogy was shot simultaneously in New Zealand. The film added so much money to the New Zealand economy (an estimated $200 million) that the country created a special minister of *Lord of the Rings*.

Screaming opossums were recorded and used for the screeches of the Orcs.

The shooting budget of the trilogy was $300 million. The advertising and marketing budget was $200 million.

YOU TALKIN' TO ME?

Robert De Niro drove a cab twelve hours a day for one month to prepare for his role in *Taxi Driver*.

Because Jodie Foster was only twelve when the movie was shot, she had to undergo hours of psychiatric evaluation by the California Labor Board before being allowed to play the part of child prostitute Iris. Her nineteen-year-old sister, Connie, was used as a body double in the "racy" scenes.

FX

The murmur of a crowd in film is recreated by having several people say "walla, walla, walla, walla."

For the 1959 Vincent Price thriller *The Tingler* theaters were rigged with buzzers under the seats to scare viewers at key moments in the film.

The movie *Earthquake* featured Sensurround, which shook the theater seats.

During the 1950s, the movie industry experimented with "smell-o-vision"—releasing odors into the theater during a film. While it never caught on, Sony has patented a newer version of the concept, where ultrasound waves would be used to stimulate various smell sites in the brains of moviegoers or game players. The use of such a technology, however, is still a long way off.

The U.S. Department of Labor prohibits newborns under the age of fifteen days from working in television or movies. That "newborn" look is created by rubbing red jam and cream cheese on older infants or premature babies over fifteen days old.

LOCKING LIPS

Eskimos don't rub noses, they kiss like everyone else. This old myth was created by a 1922 Hollywood movie about the Inuits called *Nanook of the North*.

The first movie kiss between two men took place in World War I film *Wings*, which won the first Academy Award for Best Picture, in 1927. During the war, it was common for comrades in arms to give each other fraternal kisses as a way of bonding.

DARN IT, SCARLETT!

The Motion Picture Association passed a new production code in 1939 to allow Clark Gable to use the word "damn" in *Gone With the Wind*.

Scarlett O'Hara's full name is Katie Scarlett O'Hara Hamilton Kennedy Butler.

CLOSING CREDITS

Wings (1927) and *Cavalcade* (1932) are the only movies to win the Oscar for Best Picture that are not available on DVD.

Some of the funding for *Monty Python and the Holy Grail* came from the bands Pink Floyd, Led Zeppelin, and Jethro Tull. The members of Floyd were such big *Monty Python* fans that they took breaks from recording when the television show came on.

William Randolph Hearst attempted to have a group of Hollywood directors, led by Louis B. Mayer, buy *Citizen Kane* and burn the film. When this failed, Hearst pressured theaters not to show the movie, smeared director Orson Welles in the press, and had the FBI investigate him.

United Artists was formed in 1919 by actors Charlie Chaplin, Mary Pickford, and Douglas Fairbanks; director D. W. Griffith; and attorney William Gibbs McAdoo.

A large tub of buttered popcorn contains around 1,600 calories.

Movies found on the International Space Station include *Apollo 13*, *Around the World in 80 Days*, and *So I Married an Axe Murderer*.

William Wallace and his men never wore kilts as depicted in the movie *Braveheart*. No Scots wore them at that time.

Modern movies run at twenty-four frames per second, cheap cartoons at six to eight frames per second.

CHANNEL SURFING

HARD WIRED

Cable TV was born in 1948, when Mahanoy City, Pennsylvania, appliance store owner John Walson ran a cable from an antenna on top of a mountain down to his store in the valley, so he could demonstrate his televisions to potential customers. He then ran lines to the homes of his customers that lived along the path of the cable. Walson charged one hundred dollars for the hookup and two dollars a month service fee. The company he founded—Service Electric Cable TV Inc.—is still in business today.

GREETINGS, CICELY

Northern Exposure takes place in the fictional town of Cicely, Alaska, based on Talkeetna, a town eighty miles north of Anchorage. The location shooting was done in Roslyn, Washington.

The mural for Roslyn's Café in the opening credits is from an actual café; however, the producers had to add an apostrophe "s" because the show is supposed to be in Cicely. The "s" was painted over after the show wrapped.

Elaine Miles, who played the part of Marilyn, landed the role accidentally, after she took her mother to the audition and they liked her instead. Elaine's mother, however, was cast in the part of Marilyn's mother.

Darren Burrows, who played Ed, is Cherokee and Apache Indian, but has blond hair and had to dye it for the show.

SUNSHINE CAB COMPANY

Tony Danza is driving the cab in the opening credits of *Taxi*.

After three seasons, in 1982, the show's director, James Burrows, and writers Glen Charles and Les Charles left to create *Cheers*.

Taxi was canceled by ABC in 1982 and picked up by NBC, where it ran until July 1983.

WHERE EVERYBODY KNOWS YOUR NAME

Originally, *Cheers* was to have been about an ex–football player in Barstow, California. When Ted Danson was cast as Sam Malone, they decided to make him an ex–Boston Red Sox player, due to his body type.

John Ratzenberger, who played Cliff Clavin, had auditioned for the part of Norm. When he didn't get it, he asked the producers if they had a role for a bar know-it-all. They liked the idea and hired him.

Kelsey Grammer, who played Frasier, ended up playing that character for twenty seasons (counting *Frasier*), which ties him with James Arness of *Gunsmoke* for being in the same role for the most years.

Shelley Long, who played Diane, resented Kelsey Grammer's addition to the show and tried to have him removed, but he was much too popular for that to happen.

Cheers was almost canceled when it finished seventy-seventh, or dead last, in the ratings after its first week on the air in September 1982. After surviving cancellation, it went on to become one of the most successful sitcoms of all time, airing until May 1993.

Norm's first name was Hillary. His *middle* name was Norman.

Writer/producer David Angell and his wife were both killed on September 11, 2001, when the plane on which they were traveling on from Boston to Los Angeles was hijacked and flown into the World Trade Center.

I'LL BE THERE
IN FIFTEEN MINUTES!

It takes ten and a half months to complete a season of *24*.

It only takes Jack Bauer fifteen minutes to get wherever he needs to go.

The only character, aside from Jack, to appear in all seven seasons, so far, is that of Secret Service agent Aaron Pierce, played by Glenn Morshower.

YOU'RE GONNA
MAKE IT AFTER ALL

The Mary Tyler Moore Show was originally written about a divorcee, but the network felt that was too controversial, even for liberated Mary. The show opens in 1970 with her breaking off an engagement instead.

Gavin MacLeod, who played Murray, first auditioned for the part of Lou Grant.

Jack Cassidy, who played Ted's brother, auditioned for the part of Ted.

WJM, the letters of the TV station, stand for "Wild Jack Monroe," the station's owner.

Mary Tyler Moore's real life husband, Grant Tinker, is seen having lunch with her in the opening credits of the show.

Also in the opening credits are producers James L. Brooks and Allan Burns, who are seen jogging past Mary in the park.

Mary wore a wig in the show's first season to make her look less like Laura Petrie, whom she played on *The Dick Van Dyck Show*.

Mary Tyler Moore began her acting career as "Happy Hotpoint," a little elf who danced on Hotpoint appliances in television commercials in the 1950s.

SHUTIE!

Kevin James, who plays Doug Heffernan on *The King of Queens*, also played that same character on three other CBS sitcoms—*Cosby*, *Everybody Loves Raymond*, and *Becker*.

Kevin James's parents on the show and in real life are named Janet and Joe.

James's real wife, Steffiana De La Cruz, appeared four times on the show, in four different roles. Leah Remini's husband, Angelo Pagan, also appeared in the show, six different times, in five different roles.

TOSSED SALADS AND SCRAMBLED EGGS

Frasier is the only TV show to have won five consecutive Outstanding Comedy Series Emmy awards.

The celebrities who lend their voices on Frasier's radio call-in show didn't come in to the studio to record; they simply called in their lines.

Lisa Kudrow was cast in the role of Roz, but was replaced by Peri Gilpin.

All the regular characters from *Cheers* appeared on the show, except Coach (Nicholas Colasanto, who died) and Rebecca (Kirstie Alley).

To get Moose the dog to lick Frasier's father (John Mahoney), they rubbed Mahoney's face with liver pâté.

David Hyde Pierce claims he had no interest in opera or wine before being cast as Niles. It was John Mahoney who introduced him to them.

David Hyde Pierce received a record eleven straight Emmy nominations for *Frasier*.

HOLY CRAP, MARIE!

Ray Romano's real life brother is a cop with the NYPD.

The three actors who played Ray Barone's kids on *Everybody Loves Raymond* are all siblings in real life—Madylin, Sawyer, and Sullivan Sweeten.

The closing credits always ended with a different dish of food. The final episode ended with a check and the words "No Charge."

JUST BE COS

When producers Tom Werner and Marcy Carsey approached Bill Cosby about doing *The Cosby Show*, Cosby wanted the family to be blue-collar, with Bill driving a limo and a stay-at-home mom. They convinced him to make the family much more affluent.

> *The Cosby Show* was shot in New York, because Bill Cosby didn't care for Hollywood.

ABC rejected *The Cosby Show* before it was picked up by NBC.

> The character Rudy was supposed to be a son, but when an appropriate boy wasn't found, a girl was cast.

Claire's maiden name on the show was Hanks, the same maiden name as Cosby's real life wife.

> Whitney Houston was almost cast as Sondra, the Huxtable's oldest daughter.

The actor who played Theo's friend Cockroach—Carl Anthony Payne II—was dropped from the show because he wouldn't cut his hair.

> The show's theme song, "Monk's Hat," was written by Bill Cosby and Benny Golson.

DO YOU BELIEVE IN MAGIC?

The character Samantha on *Bewitched* was originally supposed to be called Cassandra.

Jodie Foster and Helen Hunt both tried out for the part of Tabitha.

The house that was used for the exterior shots of nosy neighbor Mrs. Kravitz's is the same exterior used for *The Partridge Family* and *The Donna Reed Show*.

I Dream of Jeannie was accused of ripping off some ideas from *Bewitched*, by that show's producers. As a little jab, in one episode of *Jeannie*, Tony and Roger are working with a chimpanzee named "Sam."

Jeannie's bottle was really a decorated Jim Beam liquor decanter. (Now you know why she was so happy all the time.)

NBC had little faith in the future success of *I Dream of Jeannie* during season one, which is why they filmed it in black-and-white to save some money.

LOVE AND MARRIAGE

Married with Children was the longest running show, until *Baywatch*, to never win an Emmy award.

The fountain shown during the opening credits is Chicago's Buckingham Fountain.

The highway scene in the opening credits is taken from the 1983 movie *Vacation*. The Griswold's green, paneled station wagon can be seen on the road.

The exterior shots of the Bundys' home are of a house in Deerfield, Illinois.

The Bundy family name came from World Wrestling Federation villain King Kong Bundy.

Originally, the parts of Al and Peg were offered to Sam Kinison and Roseanne Barr.

O!

Oprah started her career at nineteen, as a news anchor at Nashville's WLAC-TV.

Oprah was voted most popular in high school.

Oprah had a baby boy when she was fourteen, but the infant died after two weeks, of complications from being two months premature.

Oprah's family was so poor that she didn't get her first pair of shoes until she was six.

A THREE-HOUR TOUR

At the very beginning of the opening credits for *Gilligan's Island*, an American flag can be seen flying at half-mast in the harbor. This is because President John F. Kennedy had just been assassinated.

The lagoon used to shoot *Gilligan's Island* was the same one used for the 1954 film *Creature from the Black Lagoon*.

The island used in the long shots shown in the opening and closing credits is one found in Kaneohe Bay, in Oahu.

Natalie Schafer, who played Mrs. Howell, had a clause in her contract forbidding close-ups.

Raquel Welch tried out for the part of Mary Ann and Jayne Mansfield for the role of Ginger. (That would have been some island to be marooned on!) Jerry Van Dyke passed on playing Gilligan.

The S.S. *Minnow* was so named as a poke at Federal Communications Commission chairman Newton Minow, who in 1964 claimed that television was "America's vast wasteland."

During the first season, Dawn Wells, who played Mary Ann, and Russell Johnson, who played the Professor, were listed simply as "the rest" in the credits, because producer Sherwood Schwartz thought they would be very minor characters. During the second season, their names were added to the credits and "the Professor and Mary Ann" was added to the end of the theme song.

Gilligan had no first name, but Sherwood Schwartz had settled on using Willie if he ever needed one.

OOPS!

Early television talk show host Faye Emerson may have had the first live wardrobe malfunction, when in 1950, her cleavage spilled out of her low-cut dress while on air broadcasting *The Faye Emerson Show*.

LAUGHTER IN A CAN

CBS engineer Charles Douglass invented canned laughter. He recorded hours of laughs and guffaws from the audiences at *The Red Skelton Show* and compiled them in his "laff box." It was first used on *The Hank McCune Show*, in 1950. Up until the early 1970s, Douglass and his machine had a virtual monopoly on television laugh tracks.

The dialogue on sitcoms with laugh tracks provides a slight pause after "funny" lines, for the insertion of laughter. When heard without the laugh track, the dialogue sounds choppy and unnatural.

MR. TELEVISION

Regis Philbin holds the Guinness record for most hours spent in front of a television camera.

He was named after his father's alma mater, Regis High School in Manhattan.

HERE'S A STORY,
OF A LOVELY LADY . . .

The Brady Bunch never made it higher than thirty-four in the ratings.

Gene Hackman was considered for the part of Mike Brady, but didn't get the role because he was an unknown at the time.

Tiger the Dog vanished after the first season, but the doghouse stayed in the "backyard" to hide a burn made in the Astroturf by a falling light.

POSTER GIRL

The iconic 1976 poster of Farrah Fawcett in the red swimsuit is the bestselling pin-up poster of all time, with 12 million copies sold.

Farrah was only paid $5,000 an episode for her one-season run on *Charlie's Angels*, but made $400,000 on her poster.

Before starring in *Charlie's Angels*, Farrah appeared in several TV commercials, for such products as Mercury Cougar, Noxema, and Ultra Brite.

Charlie's Angels had two alternate titles—*Harry's Angels* and *The Alley Cats*.

The December 1995 issue of *Playboy*, featuring Farrah

in the buff, was the magazine's top-selling issue of the 1990s.

SMILE, YOU'RE ON . . .

Allen Funt started his wacky career with a 1946 ABC radio show called *Candid Microphone*. In 1948, he jumped to television with the hidden camera show *Candid Camera*.

Woody Allen was an early writer for the show and took part in some of the gags.

A LOVELY BUNCH OF COCONUTS

Mervyn "Merv" Griffin created the two most popular syndicated television game shows—*Jeopardy!* and *Wheel of Fortune*.

Merv originally had intended to call *Jeopardy! What's the Question?*

He wrote the thirty-second piece of music that plays during Final Jeopardy. It was originally called "Time, for Tony," a lullaby he wrote for his son, Tony. Now called "Think," it has been used as the final countdown theme since the show first went on the air, in 1964.

Merv first made it big when his song "I've Got a Lovely Bunch of Coconuts" made it to the top of the Hit Parade in 1950, selling 3 million copies.

WHERE NO MAN
HAS GONE BEFORE

The first interracial kiss on television was exchanged between William Shatner and Nichelle Nichols, playing Captain Kirk and Uhura, on the original *Star Trek*.

NASA intended to name the first space shuttle *Constitution* but because of a letter writing campaign renamed it *Enterprise*.

TWO DIVORCED MEN

The Odd Couple struggled in the ratings and was canceled at the end of each of its five seasons, but was renewed after strong summer reruns ratings.

Oscar's middle name was Trevor.

The part of Oscar's ex-wife Blanche was played by Jack Klugman's real wife Brett Somers, who was separated from him at the time.

Monica Evans and Carole Shelley, who played the Pigeon sisters on the TV show, also played them in the movie.

Felix's children on the show were named Edna and Leonard. Tony Randall, who played Felix, had a sister Edna and his real first name was Leonard.

In the original Neil Simon Broadway production, Art Carney played Felix and Walter Matthau played Oscar. Jack Klugman later replaced Matthau.

BADA BING

The Bada Bing strip club in *The Sopranos* is actually a go-go club in Lodi, New Jersey, called Satin Dolls. It used to be a nightclub called Tara's.

The theme song for the show is "Woke Up This Morning," by Alabama 3.

Tony Soprano was originally going to be called the very un-Italian Tommy.

The Soprano family lives at 633 Stag Trail Road, North Caldwell, New Jersey. The house used for exterior location shots is located at 14 Aspen Drive, North Caldwell (if you care to drive by).

Ray Liotta was the top choice to play Tony, but he wouldn't commit to a TV series.

Series creator David Chase had wanted E Street Band guitarist Steve Van Zandt to play Tony, but developed the role of Silvio Dante for him after Van Zandt turned down the lead. The name comes from a short story that Van Zandt had previously written.

HBO had considered calling the show *Made in New Jersey*.

ANOTHER SHOW ABOUT NOTHING

There are no actual scripts used on *Curb Your Enthusiasm*, just plot outlines. The dialogue is improvised.

Cheryl Hines, who plays Larry's wife, only ever sees the plot outlines that pertain to her character, not the ones for what Larry is doing. This is why she looks so convincingly clueless as to the wacky situations he gets into.

The theme music for the show is from a bank commercial that got stuck in Larry David's head.

SMOKIN' FUNNY

Lucille Ball's eyebrows were shaved off for a movie she did in 1933 and they never grew back.

Lucy had miscarriages in 1942, 1949, and 1950.

Lucy was at one time the "Chesterfield Girl," a spokeswoman for the cigarette, and became hooked on them. When she did *I Love Lucy*, she kept her Chesterfields in a Philip Morris box, so as not to offend the sponsor of the show.

The word "lucky" was seldom used on *I Love Lucy*, because Philip Morris thought viewers would then think about their rival, Lucky Strikes.

T-TIME

Mr. T's real name is Laurence Tureaud.

His trademark jewelry collection came from his days of working as a nightclub bouncer. Whenever necklaces or bracelets were left behind, either by accident or during a fight, he would appropriate them.

His jewelry was eventually worth about $300,000 and took an hour to put on.

Mr. T's trademark hairdo is fashioned after that of a Mandinka warrior that he saw in an issue of *National Geographic*.

For ten years he worked as a bodyguard for several stars, charging $3,500 a day.

AND THE WINNER IS . . .

The Emmy award depicts a winged woman holding an atom. The wings symbolize the muse of art and the atom represents science.

The word "Emmy" is a feminization of "immy," a nickname for the image orthicon tubes used in early television cameras.

A BEAUTIFUL DAY IN THE NEIGHBORHOOD

Fred McFeely Rogers, aka Mister Rogers, was an ordained Presbyterian minister. He was also a vegetarian.

Fred started wearing his trademark sneakers when he found them to be quieter than shoes while working behind the set of an early television show.

THE $64 QUESTION

The origin of the expression, "That's the $64,000 question," comes from the 1940s BBS radio game show *Take It or Leave It*. A series of seven questions, increasing in difficulty, were asked of a contestant, with the final and hardest one being worth $64. This show morphed into *The $64 Question* on NBC radio in the early 1950s and later into *The $64,000 Question* on CBS television from 1955 to 1958.

NAME THAT CHARACTER

According to animator Iwao Takamoto, Scooby-Doo's name was inspired by the closing scat (dooby, dooby, doo . . .) on Frank Sinatra's hit "Strangers in the Night."

The Muppets Bert and Ernie were named after Bert the cop and Ernie the taxi driver in the 1946 movie *It's a Wonderful Life*.

Columbo's first name was "Frank."

TV TIDBITS

Danny Bonaduce became a homeless drug addict living in a car after his days on *The Partridge Family*.

Ed McMahon was once a bingo caller.

Pat Robertson's *700 Club* program was originally supported by seven hundred Christians in Portsmouth, Virginia, who each pledged a contribution of ten dollars a month, hence the name.

Keith Olbermann has restless leg syndrome, celiac disease, and a lack of depth perception that prevents him from driving.

Higgins, the dog who played Benji in the first movie, also played the dog on *Petticoat Junction*.

TAKIN' CARE OF BUSINESS

DO NOT EAT IPOD SHUFFLE

Due to frivolous lawsuits, some product warning labels seem to go a little too far. Here is a sampling of a few of the kookier warnings found on products:

iPod Shuffle—"Do Not Eat iPod Shuffle."

Motorola Razr Phone—"Don't try to dry your phone in a microwave oven."

Razor Scooter—"Warning: This product moves when used."

Extenze Male Enhancement nutritional supplement—"Do not use if pregnant or nursing."

Sea-Doo watercraft—"Never use a lit match or open flame to check fuel level."

NAME THAT COMPANY

Starbucks is named for Captain Ahab's first mate in *Moby-Dick*.

The Hard Rock Cafe restaurant chain is said to have been named after the first side of the Doors' *Morrison Hotel* album, called "Hard Rock Cafe." The chain is owned today by the Seminole tribe of Florida.

Mr. Clean is known as "Flash" in Great Britain. His first name is "Veritably."

Burger King is called Hungry Jack's in Australia.

The security firm Blackwater just changed its name to Xe, because the Blackwater name had come to symbolize out-of-control government contractors in Iraq and they felt a new name would help their image.

Google was originally called "BackRub," because the search engine used backlinks to determine how important a site was.

Yahoo began as "Jerry and David's Guide to the World Wide Web."

The oldest .com domain name is symbolics.com, registered in 1985. Symbolics was a computer manufacturer.

Kmart is named for its founder Sebastian S. Kresge.

Arby's founders, Forrest and Leroy Raffel, wanted to name their fast-food chain Big Tex, but that name was already taken. They settled on Arby's, after their initials R.B. (Raffel Brothers and roast beef).

Thom McAn shoes were named for the Scottish golfer Thomas McCann.

NEARLY NAMED

Ronald McDonald was nearly named Archie McDonald.

Little Caesars was almost named Pizza Treat.

Mrs. Paul's Kitchen was going to be named Mrs. Piszek's Kitchen.

Charmin's Mr. Whipple was almost named Edward Bartholomew, after the company president.

UP, UP, AND AWAY

The Macy's Thanksgiving Day Parade was originally held in Newark, New Jersey, in 1924, by Bamberger's department store. Macy's acquired Bamberger's in 1929 and moved the parade to New York.

The first Macy's Thanksgiving Day Parade balloon was Felix the Cat.

The balloons used to be released at the end of the parade and floated away with a return mailing address attached. Those who found the balloons could send them back to Macy's to receive a gift.

BANK ON IT

Ancient temples were the first banks because they were well built.

> Banca Monte dei Paschi di Siena, in Italy, is the world's oldest surviving bank, having been founded as a pawnshop in 1472.

In 1916, people could bring their old, dirty money to Washington, DC, to be washed and ironed.

> The Italian bank Credito Emiliano accepts eighty-five-pound Parmesan cheese wheels as collateral for loans to cheese makers. The bank has special refrigerated warehouses and trained employees to tend to the Parmesan as it ages under their care. Each wheel can be worth as a much as $425.

Friday is the most popular day of the week to rob a bank. The preferred time is between 9 a.m. and 11 a.m.

CHARGE IT

In 2008, Capital One and Wells Fargo led all credit card companies, with a profit of $2.7 million each a day. American Express made $2.3 million a day and Discover made $1.9 million. Citi did not fare as well, losing $1.5 million a day.

BULLS AND BEARS

The NASDAQ stock exchange has more trading volume than any other exchange.

NASDAQ stands for National Association of Securities Dealers Automated Quotations.

Bernie Madoff was a former chairman of the NASDAQ.

The term "blue chip," meaning high-quality stocks, originated in 1923 or 1924, when a broker first referred to high-priced stocks as being blue chips. In poker, blue chips have the highest value.

The only original member of the Dow Jones Industrial Average that is still on it is General Electric.

THE CONTEST

In 1992, Pepsi ran a contest in the Philippines offering 1 million pesos to anyone finding a bottle cap with the number 349 on it. Somehow, the company printed half a million such caps. The potential payout would have been about $18 billion. Instead, Pepsi paid out nineteen dollars per cap. The end result was not good. Pepsi still paid out $10 million, had their bottling plant attacked, and some of their execs had to flee the country.

GEE, YOU SMELL TERRIFIC

Japanese menswear maker Aoki has released deodorant shirts, socks, and underwear that eliminate body odor and kill bacteria.

Another Japanese company produces Fuwarinka rose-scented gum that not only gives people good breath but also sends a floral aroma out of body pores.

NAMES THAT STUCK

Kitty Litter is a trademark. It was introduced to the world in 1948 as the first cat litter based on clay instead of sand.

Aspirin, Band-Aid, escalator, Laundromat, and kerosene were also trademarked names when introduced.

Colgate has a trademark on the name "Tooth Fairy."

NAMES THAT SUCK

Some foreign brand names don't sound so good in English-speaking markets. A few examples follow:

A Japanese coffee creamer called Creap.

The French soft drink Pschitt.

A Finnish lock de-icer called Super Piss.

MONOLITHIC INSANITY

The word "cubicle" comes from the Latin *cubiculum*, meaning "bedchamber."

Cubicles were invented by Robert Propst in 1965 and were known at the time as the Action Office, designed to increase productivity, not increase worker density in a small space. Propst came to regret his creation, calling what it had become "monolithic insanity."

DRIVEN TO SUCCEED

Indiana was the first center of the American automobile industry, before Detroit took over that distinction.

The first electric car was made in 1834. It could go 40 miles per hour.

Swiss-born race-car driver Louis-Joseph Chevrolet and General Motors founder William C. Durant started the Chevrolet Motor Company in 1910.

The Dodge Brothers Company began making cars in 1914. They were bought out by Chrysler in 1928.

Chrysler was formed in 1925, when Walter P. Chrysler took over the Maxwell Motor Company.

Henry Ford founded the Detroit Automobile Company in 1900, which was unsuccessful. A year later he started the Henry Ford Company, but was forced out by his financial backers in 1902, when the company reorganized as Cadillac.

The 1901 Curved Dash Oldsmobile was the first affordable mass-produced car.

Ransom E. Olds, the founder of Oldsmobile, started the first automotive assembly line, in 1902, before Henry Ford.

Ransom was forced out of Olds Motor Works and started a new car company, Reo Motor Company, the name being taken from his initials.

In 1915, Ransom began selling the world's first gasoline-powered lawn mower, which he had invented.

Oldsmobile was the first car company to put a speedometer in their cars, in 1901.

Iodine was used to eliminate knocking in early cars.

The 1921 Ford Model T could run on ethanol.

In 1939, the Packard Motor Car Company made the first air-conditioned automobile.

The Toyota Corolla is the bestselling car of all time.

BIMBO, NAKED, AND LIFE DUNK

When new cars are named, an initial list of about one thousand is created by name consulting firms. The list is whittled down to about one hundred, of which only about thirty are not already patented. The car company then picks about ten names, which are consumer tested. The cost of the process, including much legal work, runs into the high six figures.

The Nissan Stanza is called the Bluebird in Japan. The 300ZX is the FairLadyZ. Other curious car names in Japan include the Daihatsu Naked, Honda Life Dunk, Toyota Deliboy, Volugrafo Bimbo, Honda That's, Isuzu Mysterious Utility, and Mitsubishi Pistachio.

The Cadillac was named after Antoine Laumet de La Mothe Cadillac, the founder of Detroit.

The Ford Mustang was named for the World War II P-51 Mustang fighter plane.

Lexus was originally going to be called Alexis (Alexis Carrington of *Dynasty* was popular at the time), but evolved into Lexus.

Prius means "to go before" in Latin.

Saturn isn't named for the planet, but for the Saturn rocket that sent men to the moon. The idea behind the name was that General Motors could beat the Japanese in the small car market, just as America had beaten the Soviets in the space race.

All Lamborghinis are named after famous bulls.

Number names for cars usually mean absolutely nothing. Often numbers are used when the company wants to emphasize the make, not the model. In the case of BMW and Mercedes, the numbers denote the engine displacement.

The Chevy "bow tie" logo is believed to have come from a French wallpaper design that company boss William C. Durant had seen in a hotel room, or it was inspired by the Swiss cross.

The BMW logo harkens back to the company's early days as an airplane manufacturer during World War I. It represents stylized white propeller blades against the blue sky.

The Toyota logo is derived from the Japanese word meaning "eight," which is considered a lucky number.

SOME NAMES ARE BETTER THAN OTHERS

The Volkswagen Touareg has the same name as an African tribe that sold slaves well into the 1900s.

The Buick LaCrosse, which was to be sold in Canada, is French-Canadian slang for masturbation.

IF YOU HAVE TO ASK
THE PRICE . . .

The base price of the Bugatti Veyron 16.4 Grand Sport roadster is $2.2 million. The car delivers 1,001 horsepower and goes from 0 to 62 miles per hour in 2.5 seconds. The seats are covered in leather that comes from cows raised in alpine meadows, above the altitude where bugs that bite can leave their marks on the hides. Alas, there are no cup holders.

The ashtrays in a Rolls-Royce empty themselves.

. . . YOU CAN'T AFFORD THE INSURANCE

The most expensive mass produced new cars to insure are usually sports cars. The more frequent and expensive the claims made by the owners of a particular model are, the higher the average annual premium. The top five 2009 models to insure were the Nissan GT-R at $2,533; the Dodge Viper at $2,446; the BMW M6 at $2,236; the Ford Shelby at $2,186; and the Mercedes-Benz G-Class at $2,088. On the other hand, the least expensive new cars to insure are typically economy cars. The five cheapest to cover in 2009 were the Hyundai Santa Fe at $832; the Kia Sportage at $840; the Hyundai Entourage at $848; the Kia Sedona at $857; and the Kia Rio5 at $870.

GEICO stands for Government Employees Insurance Company. Originally, they only insured federal employees.

The company's mascot, "Martin the Gecko," made his television debut in 1999. At the time, the Screen Actors Guild was on strike and human actors were not available, so they made up the gecko character.

Martin was originally voiced by Kelsey Grammer.

CLICK IT OR TICKET

In 1949, Nash became the first auto manufacturer to put lap seat belts in one of their models.

Volvo engineer Nils Bohlin created the three-point automotive seat belt in 1963.

Other auto companies of the time were reluctant to put seat belts in their cars, believing that consumers would think cars were unsafe if they needed them.

By 1968, all cars were required by federal law to have front seat belts.

Before New York became the first state to mandate seat belt use, in 1984, only 11 percent of American drivers were using them.

Front dual airbags were federally mandated in 1998.

Before test crash dummies were invented to test auto safety, chimps, pigs, and cadavers were used.

Truckers who text while driving are twenty-three times more likely to be involved in an accident.

TALL TALES

The Waldorf-Astoria was originally two hotels. William Waldorf Astor built his Waldorf Hotel on Fifth Avenue in 1893. Four years later, his cousin John Jacob Astor built his Astoria Hotel right next door. The two hotels were later linked by a corridor. In 1929, the hotel was sold to make room for the construction of the Empire State Building. A new Waldorf-Astoria, the largest hotel in the world at the time, was then built on Park Avenue, in 1931. After his ticker tape parade for winning four gold medals in the 1936 Olympics, Jesse Owens had to ride in the freight elevator to attend a reception in his honor, because of the hotel's segregation policy at the time.

The site of the Empire State Building was once the John Thompson farm and had a stream running across it.

Construction of the Empire State Building took 410 days. The building remained largely empty after completion, because of the Great Depression and its poor location, far from public transportation hubs. It was derisively known as the "Empty State Building." It did not turn a profit until 1950.

The spire atop the building was originally intended as a mooring mast for dirigibles, but strong updrafts made this idea rather too dangerous.

Betty Lou Oliver, an elevator operator in the Empire State Building, holds the world record for the longest elevator fall survived. On July 28, 1945, when a B-25 bomber crashed into the building between the seventy-ninth and eightieth floors, Oliver's elevator plunged seventy-five floors to the basement. She was seriously injured.

More than thirty people have jumped off the building. In 1947, a fence was erected around the terrace to curtail suicides.

In 1979, a woman jumped from the eighty-sixth floor, but was blown back into the 85th floor, only sustaining a broken hip for her effort.

Colored floodlights started illuminating the top of the structure, in 1964, to commemorate holidays, seasons, and special events. The building went black, in 2004, in observance of the death of *King Kong* actress Fay Wray.

MAIL ORDER HOUSES

Sears Catalog sold a car called the Sears Motor Buggy, between 1908 and 1912, that was to be shipped to customers. Sears discontinued selling it after realizing the cost of manufacture was more than they were making in sales. Sears again sold an auto—the Allstate—between 1952 and 1953, with limited success.

From 1908 to 1940, Sears Catalog sold roughly seventy-five thousand houses by mail. Customers could order one of some 447 different home designs available. The kits, which included everything necessary to build the house, were shipped by rail.

A typical Sears home kit weighed twenty-five tons and had thirty thousand parts.

JCPenney was started by James Cash Penney.

COFFEE, TEA, OR . . .

Before 1930, airlines only used cabin boys as stewards.

According to international safety standards, flights with less than twenty passengers don't require a flight attendant. One attendant for each fifty seats is required on larger planes.

BEST STUFF ON EARTH

Snapple was started by Hyman Golden, Arnold Greenberg, and Leonard Marsh, in Valley Stream, New York, in 1972. The name "Snapple" was introduced in 1980, when they marketed a carbonated apple juice that had a "snappy apple taste."

Many of the Snapple Facts, found on the underside of the bottle caps, are wrong. Some cap facts even contradict other cap facts.

IN YOUR FACEBOOK

Facebook was started by Harvard sophomore Mark Zuckerberg in 2004. Originally, it was only available to Harvard students. It then expanded to other colleges, and later to high schools and anyone thirteen and older.

Zuckerberg got the idea for Facebook in 2003, when he hacked into Harvard's dormitory photo ID files, posted side-by-side photos of female students, and put them on a site for users to rate their "hotness." He was nearly expelled for his efforts.

ALL A-TWITTER

During early 2006 "name-storming" sessions at the podcasting company Odeo, Twitter was going to be called Twitch, because of the way cell phones vibrate in a person's pocket. However, "twitch" does not conjure up a pleasant image, so creator Jack Dorsey looked at words in the dictionary that were close to twitch and found "twitter," meaning "a short burst of inconsequential information," which is just what tweets are.

Messages are known as "tweets," not "twits," for obvious reasons.

FILL 'ER UP

When the U.S. Supreme Court broke up Standard Oil of New Jersey's monopoly in 1911, the companies that would be known as Exxon, Mobil, Amoco, Conoco, and Sohio were formed.

> The oil company Royal Dutch Shell was named by *Fortune* magazine as the corporation with the world's largest revenues in 2009, edging out last year's champ—Wal-Mart—and ExxonMobil. ExxonMobil, however, is the company with the largest profits.

The Shell name comes from the Shell Transport and Trading Company. Its founder's father ran a seashell import business in London. On a shell-collecting trip to the Caspian Sea in 1892, the son hit on the idea of exporting lamp oil from the region and had the world's first oil tanker built.

> The Shell logo is known as the "pecten." It is based on the giant scallop—*Pecten maximus*. The red and yellow colors are taken from the flag of Spain, since early Shell service stations were built in California, a state with deep Spanish connections.

Texaco began as the Texas Fuel Company, in 1901. Its logo, a white "T" inside a red star, is a reminder of its Lone Star roots.

> At one time, Texaco was the only fuel brand sold in all fifty states.

Lukoil is the biggest oil company in Russia. It was formed by the breakup of the Soviet Union, when three state-run western Siberian oil companies were merged.

Before service stations, people bought gasoline at pharmacies.

MAGNANIMOUS MAGNATES

The $8.5 million needed to purchase the land to build the United Nations in 1949 was donated by John D. Rockefeller Jr.

Joan Kroc, heir to the McDonald's fortune, bequeathed to the Salvation Army $1.6 billion in 2004.

CHEAPSKATE

Oil heir John Paul Getty had pay phones installed in his Tudor mansion and dial locks put on the regular phones at the estate.

When Getty's grandson, John Paul Getty III, was kidnapped in 1973, he refused to give his son, John Paul Getty II, the $3.2 million ransom demanded. After the kidnappers cut off one of the grandson's ears, Getty agreed to loan his son the money, at 4 percent interest, but only after he had negotiated the price down to $2 million. Getty III was released after the ransom was paid, and the kidnappers were never caught.

MELVIN AND HOWARD

Howard Hughes suffered from obsessive-compulsive disorder, which caused him to arrange his peas by size and watch movie reels alone for four months in the nude, while subsisting on only chocolate bars and milk. He spent the latter part of his life living in different hotel penthouse suites around the world, sometimes buying the hotel to ensure that he would not be bothered by management.

After Hughes died, a suspicious will surfaced that named a Utah gas station owner—Melvin Dummar—as a recipient. Dummar claimed that he once rescued a lost and bloodied Hughes from a ditch on the side of a Nevada highway. A jury later found the will to be a forgery, Hughes having died intestate. The story was made into the 1980 film *Melvin and Howard*.

FLOODING THE COMPETITION

The flood that wiped out Johnstown, Pennsylvania, in 1889 was caused by the breach of an earthen dam built by the private sporting club of which steel magnate Andrew Carnegie was a member. Cambria Iron and Steel Company, the world's largest producer of steel and Carnegie's main competitor, was severely damaged in the flood, allowing Carnegie's company to take the lead in steel production. (Coincidence?)

J. P. MONEYBAGS

John Pierpont Morgan is credited with uttering the famous line "If you have to ask the price, you can't afford it."

He suffered from rhinophyma, which results from untreated rosacea. That gave him a huge, deformed, pitted, purple nose with bulbous nodules.

In 1895, J.P. Morgan & Company became the world's first billion-dollar corporation.

Also in 1895, J. P. Morgan personally arranged to bail out the U.S. Treasury with $60 million in gold.

On September 16, 1920, an anarchist's bomb went off in front of the J.P. Morgan & Company headquarters on Wall Street, killing thirty-eight and injuring four hundred. The perpetrators were never apprehended.

Morgan's house was the first in New York City to be fitted with electric lights.

Morgan was booked to sail on the *Titanic*, but changed his mind at the last minute.

OLD MONEY

John Jacob Astor was America's first multimillionaire. In today's dollars, he would have been the fourth richest American ever.

MICROSMART

Bill Gates was hired by his prep school to write the program for its class scheduling. He wrote the code to ensure that he was put in classes that were predominately female.

Gates scored a 1590 out of a possible 1600 on his SATs.

APPLE POLISHER

Steve Jobs was adopted. His biological father was a Syrian graduate student.

In 1978, artist Chrisann Brennan gave birth to Jobs's daughter. He denied paternity, claiming in court documents that he was sterile, and Brennan was forced to subsist on welfare. He later admitted paternity.

In 1986, Steve Jobs bought Pixar from Lucasfilm, for $10 million. He sold out to Disney in 2004, for $7.4 billion.

Jobs is a Buddhist and a vegetarian.

The earliest Apple logo featured Sir Isaac Newton sitting under an apple tree.

TAXING ISSUES

The 1915 federal tax Form 1040 had only twelve lines. It is called Form 1040 because it was the 1040th form issued by the Internal Revenue Service.

In 1921, West Virginia became the first state to enact a sales tax.

Every state has sales taxes, except Alaska, Delaware, Montana, New Hampshire, and Oregon. Hawaii calls their sales tax an excise tax, which applies to almost every business transaction, including medical bills and rent. They also allow a "tax on tax" that makes the sales tax a wacky 4.166 percent (4.712 percent in Oahu).

A female dancer—Chesty Love—was allowed to deduct the cost of her 56FF breast implants as a business expense. Unfortunately for Love, she later tripped and fell on her boobs, rupturing one.

COFFEE BREAK

The coffee break was "invented" at a Buffalo, New York, manufacturing company in 1901 or 1902.

Decaffeinated coffeepots have an orange handle, after the orange label of the original decaf coffee—Sanka—that was introduced to the United States in 1923.

DIRTY BUSINESS

Cloth diapers were first mass-produced by American Maria Allen in 1887.

The first disposable diapers were created by the Swedish paper company Pauliström in 1942.

Johnson & Johnson began selling disposable diapers in the United States in 1949. Pampers debuted in 1961.

Approximately 27 billion disposable diapers go into American landfills each year.

A GIRL'S BEST FRIEND

There are plenty of diamonds in the world. The reason the price is so high is because the major producers severely limit the supply.

In 1870, British mining companies found huge deposits in South Africa. They joined together to form De Beers Consolidated Mines Ltd. in 1888 and effectively controlled the world diamond market for the next one hundred years by limiting supply and buying up the diamonds of outside companies to keep them off the market.

Diamond engagement rings weren't that popular until De Beers started an advertising campaign in 1938 featuring celebrities of the time showing off their rocks.

The advertising slogan "A Diamond Is Forever" was coined in 1949.

By 2000, diamonds from other countries, such as Australia, Canada, and Russia, began to take a bite out of De Beers's monopoly, reducing their market share from 80 percent to 40 percent.

COIN-OP

The first vending machine was created to dispense holy water in 215 BCE.

There are 5 million parking meters in the United States.

The first Bell system outdoor pay phone was erected in Cincinnati in 1905.

At one time, there were 2.6 million pay phones in the United States.

The average American home contains ninety dollars in change.

The average coin lasts thirty years in circulation.

PITCHMEN

Willard Scott, who previously played Bozo the Clown, invented and played Ronald McDonald in television commercials that ran from 1963 thru 1966.

The only commercial Elvis Presley ever did was a 1954 radio spot for Southern Maid Donuts, in which he sang the jingle "You can get 'em piping hot after 4 p.m., you can get 'em piping hot. Southern Maid Donuts hit the spot, you can get 'em piping hot after 4 p.m." ("Four o'clock" would have been a better rhyme.)

MOVIN' ON

The first bus line in America ran between the Minnesota towns of Hibbing and Alice in 1914. Originally a one-bus operation, it grew into Greyhound Lines Inc.

The first Carnival Cruise Lines ship—*Mardi Gras*—promptly ran aground on a sandbar just off the Port of Miami on its maiden voyage, in 1972.

THANK YOU FOR SMOKING

Two former Marlboro Men died of lung cancer.

Back in the day, numerous huge stars did cigarette print ads, including Carole Lombard, Barbara Stanwyck, Lauren Bacall, and Joan Crawford. Even Jack Shea, the double gold medalist in speed skating at the 1932 Olympics, appeared in ads saying that Camels gave him the extra "pep" he needed after a tough race.

Warning labels on cigarette boxes sold in the United States became mandatory in 1965.

UNION CARDS

New York is the state with the highest rate of union membership—26.6 percent. North Carolina has the lowest at 5 percent.

More men belong to unions than women.

Full-time union workers earn an average of more than two hundred dollars per week more than their non-union counterparts.

Government employees are five times more likely to be union members than private sector workers.

LONG TIME COMING

The Concorde took fifteen years from conception to commercial use.

The typewriter took six years.

The Bose Wave music system took fourteen years.

The ballpoint pen took ten years.

It took one hundred designers three years to develop the computer game *Sims 3*.

TWENTY KEGS OF COCA-COLA

In 1911, Coca-Cola was sued by the federal government in a case known as *The United States v. Forty Barrels and Twenty Kegs of Coca-Cola*. The suit tried to force the company to remove caffeine from Coke, claiming that drinking it to excess led to young girls violating female proprieties and immorality. The court ruled in favor of the company, but the following year, Congress passed bills mandating that caffeine be listed as a deleterious, habit-forming substance in the Pure Food and Drug Act.

Most "cola" drinks today contain no cola.

FINGER LICKIN' GOOD

Only two people know the KFC chicken recipe in its entirety. It is locked in a vault in Louisville, Kentucky. Two different companies each mix one-half of the ingredients.

The name Mountain Dew is a euphemism for moonshine. The soda was invented in Knoxville, Tennessee, in the 1940s. It was originally marketed as a "zero proof moonshine" and had hillbilly characters on the labeling until 1973.

PULL A PINT

Arthur Guinness founded his brewery in Dublin when he signed an up-to-nine-thousand-year lease at forty-five pounds a year.

Isinglass, a collagen-like substance obtained from fish swim bladders, is used to clarify Guinness stout. For this reason, strict vegetarians won't drink the stuff.

LOOSE CHANGE

Wal-Mart gets sued an average of fourteen times each day.

Alexander Graham Bell's father-in-law, Gardiner Greene Hubbard, founded Bell Telephone Company and was its first president. He also was a founding member of the National Geographic Society.

Victoria's Secret stores were started in 1977, as a place where men could feel comfortable about buying lingerie.

About 19 percent of gift cards are never redeemed, according to *Consumer Reports*.

John Deere is the world's leading manufacturer of farm machinery. The company was founded by John Deere, a maker of steel plows, in 1837.

Each year, half a million workers in the United States put the Social Security number 000-00-0000 on their working papers.

Ralph Lauren never went to fashion school. He was a salesperson for Brooks Brothers and ran a tie shop, where he sold ties of his own design under the Polo label.

Levi's has sold more than 2 billion pairs of 501 jeans.

Before the invention of the paper clip, in 1867, offices used to fasten paper together with pins.

At one time, the Gerber baby was the most recognizable baby in the world. It still may be.

It is illegal to use the American flag in advertising. This law is rarely enforced.

GREAT IDEAS

The baby bottle was patented in 1841.

The first electric iron was patented in 1882 and weighed fifteen pounds.

The ballpoint pen inspired Ban Roll-on in 1952.

Toothbrushes had bristles taken from the back of a boar's head up until 1938, when DuPont introduced nylon.

In 1980, Tyson Foods bred a special chicken just for McNuggets; it's called "Mr. McDonald."

WALK ON THE WILD SIDE

BUG OFF

Insects have six legs, arachnids have eight.

Eighty percent of the world's insects live in jungles.

The world's longest insect is the twenty-two-inch stick insect found in Borneo and Malaysia.

Some insects, like the Apache cicada, can sweat to cool down.

NOT SO STUPID INSECT TRICKS

The male green-veined white butterfly injects oil of wintergreen into the female, along with his sperm, to ward off any other amorous males.

The male orb-weaving spider is just a tiny fraction of the size of the female. When he inserts his sperm packet and palp (a sexual appendage), his heart immediately stops and he dies. His palp remains swollen in the female and prevents other suitors from penetration.

When a parasitic wasp stings the spider *Plesiometa argyra*, it deposits its larvae. The spider then proceeds to spin a custom-made cocoon for the little worms, which they move into after killing the accommodating spider.

The *Glyptapanteles* parasitic wasp implants its larvae in caterpillars, which turns the caterpillar into a bodyguard for the larvae. When they emerge and attach to the plant the caterpillar is feeding on, it will defend them against predators.

WIGGLERS

Caterpillars have four thousand muscles.

Velvet worms shoot two streams of glue up to thirty centimeters long at their prey to entangle them. When the glue hardens, the worms eat the victim and the glue.

Venomous Venezuelan centipedes, which grow up to thirteen centimeters in length, hang down from cave ceilings and catch bats in mid-flight.

One type of midge larvae can live for three days in liquid nitrogen (−321°F).

WORM CALLERS

In Florida, men called "worm grunters" use wooden stakes driven into the ground to "call" worms. They rub an iron bar across the top of the stakes to vibrate the ground and produce a grunting sound. This bizarre method causes worms by the hundreds to come to the surface, where they are collected and sold as bait.

There are up to 8 million worms in the soil of each hectare of forest.

NIGHT LIGHTS

The firefly, or "lightning bug," is the state insect of Pennsylvania and Tennessee.

The light of a firefly may be green, yellow, or red.

Some firefly species mimic the light patterns of other firefly species to lure the males, which are then eaten.

Some firefly populations will flash in precise unison.

A firefly larva is known as a glowworm.

"ANT"ICS

Protomognathus americanus ants will raid the colonies of the smaller *Temnothorax* ant, take the smaller ants back to their colony, and force them to tend their young.

Some ants build structures with holes on tree branches, in which they hide. When an unsuspecting larger insect lands there, they pounce.

Ants herd aphids to the best spots for feeding on plants and protect them so they can drink the sweet honeydew the aphids exude from their recta. The ants will milk the aphids by stroking them with their antennae.

Ants in Peru will kill other plant species with formic acid in an area around the trees that they live on, so more can grow.

Carpenter ants hit their heads on wood to communicate.

Only, ants, humans, and crows fight battles in formations.

THANKS FOR THE LIFT

Botflies will catch smaller houseflies and glue their eggs onto them. When the houseflies land on a cow to drink its sweat, the cow's body warmth causes the eggs to quickly hatch and drop onto the cow. The larvae latch onto the cow with hooks and burrow under its skin, where they will feed for three months.

WHAT'S EATING YOU?

There are four thousand species of termite.

Not all termites eat wood. Some like soil, grass, or

animal droppings. Others "cultivate" a fungus as a food source.

A termite queen will lay thirty thousand eggs a day for up to twenty years.

The number of termites in a colony can reach into the millions.

WORLDWIDE WEBS

Spiders don't get caught in their own webs because they have special oils on their feet.

A sixty-acre web, built by millions of spiders, was found in 2002 on a farm in British Columbia.

North American female bola spiders suspend a sticky droplet at the end of a line of silk that they swing through the air to capture passing male moths. The moths are attracted by a pheromone the spiders produce which is similar to that of a female moth.

TICKED OFF

Ticks can ingest a blood meal of six hundred times their unfed body weight.

Hundreds of proteins in a tick's saliva numb the pain of their bite, inhibit swelling, and prevent blood clotting, allowing them to feed undetected for days.

These proteins change daily to thwart the host's immune system from developing antibodies to them.

BLUE BLOODS

Horseshoe crab blood is blue. This is because it uses copper to carry oxygen, as opposed to iron, which carries oxygen in red-blooded animals. Many other crustaceans also have blue blood; some worms have green blood; and cockroaches have clear blood.

Horseshoe crab blood, which is used by the pharmaceutical industry to test drugs for bacterial toxins, sells for up to fifteen thousand dollars a quart.

Horseshoe crabs can live up to one week out of the water.

Horseshoe crabs are more closely related to scorpions and spiders than crabs.

SNAKE EYES

Arboreal snakes have better eyesight than burrowing snakes.

The world's shortest snake is the four-inch-long Barbados threadsnake.

The tiger keelback is an Asian snake that obtains its venom from the poisonous toads that it eats.

There are no poisonous snakes, only venomous ones. (A venom is a toxin that is harmful when injected. A poison is one that is injurious upon contact or ingestion.)

Snake venom is a kind of saliva.

A prehistoric snake named *Titanoba* weighed more than 2,500 pounds, was forty-two feet long, and could swallow a full-grown alligator.

Mating is so fierce in garter snakes that more than one hundred males may try to copulate with a single female at the same time, resulting in a large writhing ball of snakes.

THE BIG STORY

Sperm whales are named for the milky white, waxy substance—spermaceti—found inside their heads, which used to be mistaken for sperm.

Sperm whales can dive to 9,800 feet in search of prey.

Their clicking noises are the loudest sounds made by any animal.

Female sperm whales care for their calves for up to ten years.

It is believed that an elephant's trunk contains between 40,000 and 100,000 individual muscles.

An elephant is able to pick up a single blade of grass with its trunk.

If an elephant wants food that is too high up in a tree to reach, it will shake the tree to dislodge it or simply knock the whole tree down.

Elephants will greet each other by clasping trunks, similar to a human handshake.

THE LONG AND SHORT OF IT

The sperm of the seed shrimp can be up to ten times the length of the shrimp itself. By comparison, a human male's sperm are about 1/30,000 of his height.

Shrimp that live around the deep ocean thermal vents grow bacteria under their backs that they eat.

NECROPHILIAC LESBIANS?

Microscopic aquatic creatures known as bdelloid rotifers are all female and haven't had sex for 300 million years. They can withstand being dried out for years on end, which causes their cell walls to rupture and their DNA to fragment. When they rehydrate, these animals re-form themselves, often incorporating DNA from other rotifers. This is essentially their form of sex (genetic re-shuffling). Since they are getting new DNA from other dead female rotifers, they have been referred to by some as "necrophiliac lesbians."

SUCKERS

Octopus arms typically have about two hundred suckers each.

Suckers are an octopus's primary means of touching and tasting things in its environment.

When threatened, octopuses can detach an arm, which will wiggle around and confuse an enemy. Detached limbs will regrow in a few months' time.

The North Pacific giant octopus can have an arm span of fourteen feet.

After her eggs have hatched, a female octopus will die.

The blue-ringed octopus, which lives in the tidal pools of northern Australia, produces venom that is fatal to humans, for which there is no antidote.

At low tide, some octopuses will leave the water and move between tidal pools.

The male paper nautilus has a penis that will detach and swim under its own power to the female.

FISH TALES

The sunflower starfish measures three feet across.

Nomura's jellyfish, found off the coast of Japan, grow to six feet in diameter and weigh in at 450 pounds.

Some fish communicate by farting.

The guppy is named for Englishman Robert John Lechmere Guppy, who discovered the fish in Trinidad in 1866.

NAME THAT FISH

Since fish populations have been greatly reduced in the last couple of decades, the seafood industry has come up with some more appetizing names for new species to make them more marketable. Some notable examples follow:

Orange roughy used to be known as slimehead. This is because of the numerous mucous canals found on its head. Orange roughys can live to be one hundred years old (so that frozen filet in your freezer could be older than grandpa).

The Patagonian toothfish is marketed in the United States as Chilean sea bass. They are not only found off the coast of Chile, but in any of the cold ocean waters north of Antarctica.

Monkfish has been sold as goosefish.

Peekytoe crabs used to be known as Maine rock crabs, a throwaway by-product of the Maine lobster industry. In 1997, they were marketed under their local nickname "peekytoe" and sold as a gourmet item.

SING LIKE A CANARY

Canaries take thirty mini-breaths per second.

Nightingales are named for their prodigious singing abilities. They will warble up to three hundred courtship songs, both day and night.

Cowbirds can sing up to forty different notes, some inaudible to humans.

Marsh warblers mimic the calls of seventy other birds.

Brown thrashers can have a repertoire of two thousand different songs.

The song of New Zealand's male kakapo can be heard four miles away.

The chaffinch may sing its song a half million times in a season.

Vinkenzetting is a sport in Belgium where thousands of chaffinches compete to see which can sing the most songs in an hour. About thirteen thousand human enthusiasts, called vinkeniers, participate.

There once was a budgie (small parrot) named Victor who had a vocabulary of more than one thousand words. (More than some people know.)

A LOT TO CROW ABOUT

The world's oldest crow is estimated to be 118 years old.

Crows use three hundred different calls.

Ravens and crows are in the same genus. Ravens are much bigger than crows. They have pointed wing tips, while a crow's are blunt and splayed. Ravens also have long, wedge-shaped tails, while a crow's is fan-shaped. In addition, a raven's beak is curved, where a crow's is flatter.

Birds in the crow family are said by scientists to be the smartest.

Carrion crows at a university in Japan collect walnuts from a tree near a traffic light. When the light turns red, the crows place the nuts in the crosswalk, waiting for cars to drive over them, and then fly in after to eat the cracked nuts.

Clarke's nutcrackers, a kind of North American crow, will collect up to thirty thousand pine seeds in the fall and bury each somewhere in an area two hundred miles square. Over the next eight months, these clever birds are able to retrieve up to 90 percent of their stash, even when the seeds are buried under several feet of snow.

Crows will watch squirrels bury a nut and swoop in to dig it up as soon as the squirrel leaves.

HOOTERS

Some owls hunt during the day.

> Owls have serrations on the leading edge of their feathers that reduce noise and make the flapping of their wings almost silent.

Owls swallow their prey whole and regurgitate the bones, fur, and other indigestible parts in pellets.

> The great gray owl hunts by sound alone. Using super-stereo hearing, the owl can detect an unsuspecting lemming and pluck it from beneath the snow with incredible accuracy.

BIRD FEEDERS

A sand grouse needs to eat from five thousand to eighty thousand seeds a day to survive. As such, it is the fastest eating bird, consuming several seeds a second.

> The ancient murrelet is the bird that spends the least amount of time on land. It lives at sea and only returns to land to lay its eggs. These birds do not even return to land to feed their young, but instead coax their two-day-old chicks to swim five miles out to sea, where they are fed.

Brünnich's guillemots, an arctic seabird, can dive to depths of up to five hundred feet beneath the ocean's surface in search of food.

HOME TWEET HOME

The male European house wren will build up to twelve nests to entice a female.

The female hornbill lays her eggs in a tree hollow and seals herself up inside for the duration, relying on her mate to supply food through a small slit.

The Australian yellow-faced honeyeater will pull fur from the back of a koala to line its nest.

The hammerkopf, a storklike bird, builds a nest six feet across.

The rufous woodpecker builds its nest in the middle of an ant colony. The ants soon get used to the nest, but will attack any intruder trying to get to the bird's eggs.

The rufous naped wren employs a similar strategy to protect its eggs, building its nest next to a wasp's nest.

A developing American white pelican chick will make loud noises from within the egg to tell its parents when it is too hot or cold. The adults then adjust the egg's incubation accordingly.

Each female cuckoo specializes in producing eggs that mimic the appearance of one specific species of bird, which she lays in the other bird's nest for that bird to unwittingly raise as her own.

A female cowbird will lay her eggs in the nest of another songbird. She will keep an eye on her eggs from a distance. If they are removed, she will quickly destroy the eggs laid by the songbird and wait for a new batch to be laid.

Contrary to popular myth, if humans handle an egg or baby bird and put it back in the nest, its mother will never know. Most birds have a very poor sense of smell.

FOR THE BIRDS

Emus don't fly, but they do migrate, by walking up to three hundred miles or more in search of rain.

There are estimated to be about 1.5 billion red-billed queleas—a small sub-Saharan bird. Flocks have been reported that are so big they take five hours to pass overhead.

An albatross can live to be sixty years old.

The common poorwill of North America hibernates during winter.

Fossil evidence seems to show that *T. rex* and other dinosaurs in the theropod family were covered with feathers.

ALIEN INVASION!!!

A group of one hundred starlings from Europe were released in Central Park by the American Acclimatization Society in 1890 and 1891. The society's goal was to release in America all the birds mentioned in Shakespeare's plays, to make European immigrants feel more at home. Those one hundred starlings (mentioned in *Henry IV*, Part 1) went on to spread across the country and become a major pest, displacing countless native birds. The U.S. Department of Agriculture currently has a program to eradicate nuisance flocks of starlings. Like the starlings, all of the house sparrows in the United States today descend from a few of these European birds released in Central Park in 1850.

The gypsy moth was brought to America in 1868 by French scientist Leopold Trouvelot, to hybridize with native silk-spinning caterpillars. He left a jar of the little critters on the windowsill of his Medford, Massachusetts, laboratory and they escaped. The moths now are the worst hardwood forest pest in the East—defoliating up to 13 million acres a year. During heavy infestations, the noise of their chewing leaves and falling excrement sounds like rain in the forest.

Dutch elm disease is a fungus introduced to the United States on imported logs from Holland in 1928. It has since decimated the native elm population.

Another nasty fungal disease of trees is chestnut blight, which came to the United States on imported wood around 1900. By 1940, there were no more mature American chestnut trees left alive.

A BREED APART

The Saluki dog was bred in Mesopotamia around 3000 BCE.

Pekinese were bred for the emperors of China and lived within the Forbidden City. For anyone injuring or killing one of these dogs, the penalty was death.

Bloodhounds get their name from being carefully bred in medieval monasteries from pure bloodstock.

Chihuahuas were raised by the Aztecs for sacrificial purposes and for food.

PAMPERED PETS

Toy poodles were once used as hand warmers by the aristocracy.

French poodles were first bred in Germany as water retrievers.

The name "poodle" derives from the German *pudeln*, meaning "to splash in water."

The distinctive "poodle clip" was designed by hunters to help the dogs move through the water more easily. The patches of hair left on the body were to protect the joints and organs from the cold.

Poodles don't shed or have dander.

HOLY HOUNDS

St. Bernards never carried casks of brandy to the snowbound, but they did locate those lost in an avalanche and dig them out. The dogs worked in male-female pairs. Both would dig victims out. The female would lie next to them to keep them warm, while the male would go for help.

St. Bernards are named for the hospice at Great St. Bernard Pass in the Swiss Alps that was run by Augustinian monks. One dog named Barry is famed for having saved more than forty people.

The St. Bernards of today are much different than the original rescue dogs. Most of the breeding stock of these dogs was killed off in a series of avalanches between 1816 and 1818. To replenish the breed, the remaining dogs were crossbred with Newfoundlands in the 1850s. However, the resulting dogs' long coats would freeze and weigh them down, making them inefficient rescue dogs.

A St. Bernard can weigh more than 260 pounds.

DOG TAILS

Dogs put their tail between their legs when scared to hide their scent glands.

Dogs have about one billion olfactory (smell) receptors. People only have 40 million.

A dog's tongue increases in size when the dog exercises, because of increased blood flow. The wet tongue hanging out of its mouth is cooled by the air, which in turn cools the blood.

Some dogs can be trained to predict an epileptic seizure in their owners. Other dogs can sense low sugar levels in diabetics and warn them so that they can ingest carbohydrates to avoid passing out.

It is estimated that 5 million pet dogs suffer from separation anxiety and many are medicated to calm them down.

TOP DOG

In the eleventh century, a dog named Saur was declared king of Norway for three years. The recently deposed human king returned to power and decreed his dog king to spite his subjects.

In 2009, a Mrs. Wang of China bought a Tibetan mastiff, which she named Yangtze River Number Two, for the record price of $582,000.

DOGGIE TREATS

A single gene mutation that may have occurred thirty thousand years ago is found in almost all short-legged dogs, like basset hounds, dachshunds, corgis, etc.

Four in ten American households have a dog. Three in ten have a cat.

More than 1 million dogs and cats have been made primary will beneficiaries in the United States since they began keeping track of these things.

The American Kennel Club Museum of the Dog is located in West St. Louis County, Missouri.

In 2008, a Florida couple had their yellow lab Lancelot cloned into a new, genetically identical puppy.

The average city dog lives three years longer than the average country dog.

MEOW

There are about fifty breeds of cats.

In parts of Europe, a black cat crossing your path is considered *good* luck.

Forty percent of cats are ambidextrous, the rest are either left-pawed or right-pawed.

Cats have thirty-two muscles that control outer ear movements.

Cats lose as much moisture through saliva used during grooming as they do through urination.

There are only three animals that walk by stepping with both legs of the same side at the same time (both right legs step, then both left legs step)—the camel, the giraffe, and the cat.

HORSING AROUND

In wild horses it's the mares, not the stallions, that determine where the herds go.

Horses were probably first domesticated in the Ukraine or Kazakhstan around six thousand years ago.

There are more than three hundred breeds of horse.

Horses have a blind spot directly in front of their eyes, from about four feet away until six inches near their face. They cannot see the ground near their feet or their chests. This is why they may back away if patted between their eyes.

Horses have the largest eyes of any land mammal. Their field of vision is more than 350 degrees.

Some of the best violin bows are made from horse-tail hairs.

The lifespan of a domestic horse is from twenty-five to thirty years.

A colt is a male horse under the age of four.

A filly is a female horse under the age of four.

A mare is a female over four.

A stallion is a non-castrated male over four.

A gelding is a castrated male over four.

A horse's hoof is made of the same material as the human fingernail. Like fingernails, hooves continue to grow, and need to be trimmed every five to eight weeks.

Horses can sleep standing up or lying down. They take many short naps while standing up, and only need to lie down one or two hours every few days to get enough deep sleep to keep them healthy.

There is only one small population of truly wild (never domesticated) horses—Przewalski's Horse, living today in Mongolia.

A SMUCK OF JELLYFISH

There are many interesting, although little known, collective nouns for groups of animals. Here is a sampling:

An array is a group of hedgehogs.

An ambush is a group of tigers.

A badelynge is a group of ducks on the ground.

A barren is a group of mules.

A business is a group of ferrets.

A cast is a group of hawks, falcons.

A clutter is a group of spiders.

A convocation is a group of eagles.

A covert is a group of coots.

A descent is a group of woodpeckers.

A dole is a group of turtles.

A down is a group of hares.

An earth is a group of foxes.

An erst is a group of bees.

An exaltation is a group of larks in flight.

A fling is a group of oxbirds, sandpipers.

A float is a group of crocodiles.

A grist is a group of bees.

A kindle is a group of kittens.

A knab is a group of toads.

A labor is a group of moles.

A leap is a group of leopards.

A murmuration is a group of starlings.

A muster is a group of peacocks.

A mute is a group of hounds.

A paddling is a group of ducks in water.

A pump is a group of ducks in flight.

A rafter is a group of turkeys.

A roost is a group of pigeons.

A skein is a group of geese in flight.

A skulk is a group of foxes.

A sleuth is a group of bears.

A sloth is a group of bears.

A smuck, or smack, is a group of jellyfish.

A sord is a group of wildfowl.

A stud is a group of mares.

A sute is a group of bloodhounds, wildfowl.

A tiding is a group of magpies.

A tower is a group of giraffes.

A tribe is a group of goats.

A troubling is a group of goldfish.

An unkindness is a group of ravens.

A venue is a group of vultures.

A volery is a group of birds.

A watch is a group of nightingales.

A yoke is a group of oxen.

MAMMAL MEMOS

All mammals have fur, sweat glands, and three middle ear bones for hearing.

Most mammals are red-green colorblind.

Platypuses and spiny anteaters are the only mammals that don't have a belly button.

Raccoons are the leading carriers of rabies in the United States, followed by bats, skunks, and foxes. Dogs are way down on the list.

Kangaroo rats never drink water. They extract moisture from the seeds they eat.

A rat species that grows to thirty-two inches long was discovered in Papua New Guinea in 2009.

The tenrac, a hedgehog-like animal from Madagascar, has twenty-two to twenty-four nipples.

The canine teeth (tusks) of the babirusa, or pig-deer, of Indonesia, grow straight through the roof of its mouth and can continue to grow and curve back into the pig's brain.

Shrews have a larger brain-to-body ratio than humans.

A giant panda weighs four ounces at birth, 1/900th of the mother's weight.

While roosting, bats and some birds let their temperature drop to the surrounding air temperature.

Naked mole rats cannot regulate their body temperature, but assume the temperature of their burrows, typically 86°F.

It requires sixty female or thirty-five male minks to make a coat.

Since 1970, there have been seventy mountain lion attacks in the United States.

The tree-dwelling sloths are slow movers in more ways than one. They only defecate once every eight days and come down to the ground to do so.

LEAVE IT TO BEAVERS

Water lilies are a North American beaver's favorite food.

Beavers build a lodge by sinking vertical poles into the river bottom, intertwining horizontal branches, and filling in the gaps with leaves and mud.

Beavers build at night.

Beavers slap the surface of the water with their tails to warn others of danger.

The beaver lodge has an underwater entrance and two rooms, one for drying off and the other where the family lives.

Up until thirteen thousand years ago, there were giant beavers in North America that were eight feet long.

The Yupik Eskimos used dried beaver testicles to relieve pain.

In the 1600s, the Catholic Church ruled that beaver meat was "fish," and as such could be eaten on Fridays during Lent.

HOT PLANTS

Skunk cabbage begins to grow in early spring, often while still covered with snow. The plant is able to generate enough heat through cellular respiration to melt the frozen ground. Its flower head can maintain a temperature of 70°F for two weeks when the outside air is much colder.

Windmill palm trees can survive in temperatures as low as 5°F. Many others are hardy down to 15°F.

THE GRASS IS ALWAYS GREENER

There are 32 million acres of lawn in the United States, roughly the size of Pennsylvania, making grass the number one grown "crop."

Kentucky bluegrass is green like other grasses. Its flower buds, however, are bluish when the grass is allowed to grow tall. Most bluegrass seed comes from farms in the Pacific Northwest.

On a hot day, lawns can be twenty degrees cooler than bare dirt and forty degrees cooler than cement.

SEEDY STATS

The largest seeds in the world weigh fifty-five pounds and come from the double coconut palm. The smallest seeds come from tropical orchids and weigh 10 billionths of an ounce.

Nectarines are simply peaches with a smooth skin. They can spontaneously arise from a peach tree.

Softwood trees can be harder than hardwood trees.

Poison ivy contains an allergenic oil, not a poison.

There are about 250 different species of trees in a single hectare of tropical rain forest.

The magnolia is named after French botanist Pierre Magnol.

There are olive trees in the Garden of Gethsemane that were around at the time of Christ.

There is a small, cranberry-like fruit that, when chewed, afterward makes any sour food taste sweet. This taste bud–altering effect lasts fifteen to thirty minutes. Known as "miracle fruit," these West African fruits make lemons taste like candy and oranges disgustingly sweet.

WORD WISE

WORDSMITHS

Jack London was the first American novelist to earn a million dollars.

Jane Austen never married.

The first American to win the Nobel Prize in Literature was Sinclair Lewis, in 1930, primarily for his novel *Babbitt*.

Herman Melville, author of *Moby-Dick*, worked briefly on a whaling ship, before deserting it in the Marquesas Islands.

Alex Haley, the bestselling African American author in history, was sued for plagiarizing *The African*, by Harold Courlander, when writing *Roots*. After a 1978 trial, Haley made a $650,000 settlement payment to Courlander.

F. Scott Fitzgerald was born Francis Scott Key Fitzgerald, named after his famous relative Francis Scott Key, writer of the words to the American national anthem, but he was referred to as Scott.

The Tom Wolfe novel *The Bonfire of the Vanities* originally ran as a twenty-seven-installment serial in *Rolling Stone* magazine in 1984–85. Wolfe chose this method of publishing because he felt that the pressure of a deadline would help him overcome a case of writer's block he was experiencing. Wolfe was paid $750,000 for the film rights to the book, but the 1990 movie, starring Tom Hanks, bombed.

> *Uncle Tom's Cabin*, by Harriet Beecher Stowe, was the bestselling novel of the nineteenth century.

At 1,777 lines, *The Comedy of Errors* is Shakespeare's shortest play.

CATCHER IN HIDING?

Published in 1951, *The Catcher in the Rye* still sells about 250,000 copies a year. It has sold 65 million copies worldwide.

> *Catcher* holds the distinction of having been the most censored book in the United States, as well as the most taught in high schools after *Of Mice and Men*.

J. D. Salinger dated Eugene O'Neill's daughter Oona, who later married Charlie Chaplin.

> *The New Yorker* rejected the first seven short stories Salinger sent them.

Salinger has become a recluse, not having published anything since 1965.

Sean Connery's character in the movie *Finding Forrester* is based on Salinger.

PAPA

When Ernest Hemingway was wounded by mortar and machine gun fire during World War I, he stuffed cigarette butts into his wounds to stop the bleeding.

He gave himself the nickname "Papa" when he was twenty-seven.

Hemingway became such good friends with F. Scott Fitzgerald that Fitzgerald's wife, Zelda, accused them of being lovers. To convince her otherwise, Fitzgerald had sex with a prostitute.

Hemingway committed suicide, as did his father, two of his siblings, and granddaughter Margaux Hemingway.

"SHORT" STORY

William Faulkner was born William Cuthbert Falkner. The story goes that when his first book was published, the typesetter made the spelling error and he let it go.

Faulkner tried to join the U.S. Army to fight in World

War I, but at five feet, five and a half inches, he was too short to enlist.

NOT THE CANDY BAR

O. Henry, born William Sidney Porter, coined the term "banana republic" in his novel *Cabbages and Kings*, written in Honduras, while he was on the lam from American authorities. Upon his return to the United States, he was arrested for embezzling money from a bank he worked for and sent to prison for three years. While serving his time in the Ohio Penitentiary, he adopted the pen name O. Henry, supposedly taken from the first two letters in Ohio and the second, third and last two in penitentiary.

LORD OF THE W'S

J.R.R. Tolkien's first writing job was with *The Oxford English Dictionary*. He was responsible for the etymology and history of words of Germanic origin, starting with the letter "W."

Tolkien wrote *The Hobbit* as a story for his children.

PUPPIES AND PIGS

The bestselling children's books of all time, as of 2000, according to *Publishers Weekly*, were *The Pokey Little Puppy*, by Janette Sebring Lowery, in hardcover; and *Charlotte's Web*, by E. B. White, in paperback.

Four years before *Charlotte's Web* was published, White had a book published called *Death of a Pig*. It recounted his failure to save a sick pig from slaughter. *Charlotte's Web* was his attempt to right that wrong.

A. A. Milne created his *Winnie the Pooh* stories from his son Christopher Robin Milne's stuffed animal collection, which included a bear named Winnie the Pooh. Milne's farmstead in Ashdown Forest, East Sussex, England, was the setting for his stories.

Dr. Seuss liked to wear zany hats to parties.

WIZARDS AND MUGGLES

Harry Potter author J. K. Rowling has stated that the word "Voldemort" should be pronounced (if you dare!) with a silent "t."

According to Rowling, the Hogwarts name probably came to her mind as a result of having seen the plant hogwort at Kew Gardens (botanical gardens in London).

Hagrid is derived from the term "hagridden," meaning to torment or harass, especially with worry or dread.

Dursley is a small town near where Rowling was raised.

Snape is named for a town in Suffolk. The character is based on a former chemistry teacher that Rowling wasn't very fond of.

Dumbledore means "bumblebee" in Old English.

Rowling insisted that the cast of the movies all be British. Liam Aiken, who was originally cast as Harry, worked one day on the movie, before being fired for not being British.

Rowling personally picked actors Robbie Coltrane (Hagrid) and Alan Rickman (Snape). Six-foot-ten-inch former English rugby player Martin Bayfield was Coltrane's body double.

To keep true to the books, Daniel Radcliffe (Harry) wore green contacts and Emma Watson (Hermione) was fitted with buckteeth. When it was realized that Daniel's eyes wouldn't stop tearing and Emma couldn't speak properly, they were dropped.

Radcliffe's first movie role was in 2001's *Tailor of Panama*.

Radcliffe is now the richest teenager in England.

The last four books in the *Harry Potter* series each became the fastest selling book in history when it was released.

J. K. Rowling had wanted the first *Harry Potter* novel published using her real name—Joanne Rowling. Her publisher felt that the target audience of young boys might not go for a book written by a woman, so she used her first initial and that of her paternal grandmother's first name ("K" for Kathleen). Rowling's friends know her as "Jo."

Her editor advised her not to quit her day job, as she would never make a living writing children's books. She became the first person to become a billionaire (in U.S. dollars) writing books.

WHODUNNIT?

Agatha Christie never attended any public or private schools, but was taught at home by a tutor.

Christie at one time worked in a pharmacy, which gave her insights for the many mysteries she wrote about poisonings.

Sir Arthur Conan Doyle was Scottish, not English.

Conan Doyle was a bored doctor, writing his Sherlock Holmes mysteries during the long stretches between patients.

Doyle, in the style of Holmes, investigated two closed criminal cases and had the accused men vindicated.

Doyle also wrote science fiction stories featuring Professor Challenger as the protagonist.

LIFE WITH HILLARY

Hillary Clinton's 2003 memoir *Living History* was the fastest selling nonfiction book up until that time, moving 200,000 copies its first day on sale. Simon & Schuster had paid her an $8 million advance, a near record at the time. She signed over twenty thousand copies and required icing and wrist support treatments afterward.

Sarah Palin's 2009 book, *Going Rogue*, beat out Hillary, selling 300,000 copies on its first day on sale, and 700,000 copies in the first week.

BON APPETIT!

Julia Child's magnum opus *Mastering the Art of French Cooking* once again became a number one bestseller in 2009, forty-nine years after its publication, due to the great reception of the movie *Julie & Julia*. Sales in one week in August 2009 were twenty-two thousand copies, more than in any previous week since its publication. Child and her collaborators finished Volume 1 in 1960 and Volume 2 in 1970. Her second volume covered baking and bread making much more extensively.

Julie Powell, author of the book *Julie & Julia: 365 Days, 524 Recipes, 1 Tiny Apartment Kitchen*, wrote the book from her experience writing the blog The Julie/Julia Project. It was the first blog to ever be made into a movie. Her second book, *Cleaving: A Story of Mar-*

riage, Meat, and Obsession, is about how she cheated on her husband after the success of her first book.

THE GOOD BOOK

The Bible doesn't specify the number of wise men. Only Matthew mentions them and he simply says they brought three gifts.

The first Gideon's Bible was placed in a hotel room in Superior, Montana, in 1908.

The Bible has been translated into 2,200 languages and dialects.

ELLE NUMERO UNO

Elle Macpherson has appeared on the most *Sports Illustrated* swimsuit issue covers—five.

Elle, which means "she" in French, is the world's largest fashion magazine, with thirty-nine international editions.

BUNNY BUSINESS

Oddly, Hugh Hefner worked as the circulation manager for *Children's Activities* magazine in 1953, just before he launched *Playboy.*

Hefner has a species of rabbit (what else?) named after him—*Sylvilagus palustris hefneri.*

Hef is strongly anti-drugs. Anyone found using them at the Mansion is permanently banned. (Wanton nudity and sex don't seem to be a problem, though.)

Hefner owns the burial vault next to Marilyn Monroe's. Anna Nicole Smith's sister contacted Hef days after her death and asked him if he would sell the plot, so Anna could be buried next to her idol. Hefner declined.

FUNNY BUSINESS

The comic strip *Peanuts* was originally called *Li'l Folks* by Charles Schulz, but the name was too close to other strips—*Li'l Abner* and *Little Folks*—so United Features Syndicate chose *Peanuts*, after the peanut gallery on *Howdy Doody*. Schulz always hated the name.

Peanuts is called *Small Fry* in the Netherlands and *Radishes* in Denmark.

Peppermint Patty's "real" name is Patricia Reinhardt.

THE BUMSTEADS

Blondie debuted in 1930. The comic strip ran as a series of films from 1938 to 1950 and as a radio series from 1939 to 1950.

Blondie's maiden name was Boopadoop (from the flapper phrase "boop-boop-a-doop").

Blondie was a 1930s flapper, who married wealthy Dagwood Bumstead. Unfortunately, Dagwood's rich father disowned him for marrying Blondie and he was forced to go to work for the J. C. Dithers Construction Company.

Dagwood's son Alexander was born Baby Dumpling.

Early on, the strip featured Blondie, but more recently Dagwood is the main protagonist.

Dagwood's propensity for eating huge, multilayered sandwiches, held together with a toothpick topped with an olive, led to the word "Dagwood" entering *Webster's New World College Dictionary* for that type of sandwich.

In 2006, Dean Young, son of the strip's creator, Chic, began opening a series of Dagwood Sandwich Shoppes.

COWABUNGA

Artists Peter Laird and Kevin Eastman, using money from a tax refund and a loan from Eastman's uncle, created *The Teenage Mutant Ninja Turtles* as a one-off parody of several different early 1980s comic books. *The Turtles* became phenomenally successful, spinning off numerous TV series, movies, video games, toys, and food lines.

VERY PUZZLING

Arthur Wynn created the first published crossword puzzle for the *New York World* Sunday newspaper in 1913.

Sudoku was inspired by "Latin squares," invented by Swiss mathematician Leonhard Euler, in 1783. The modern numbers puzzle was devised by American architect Howard Garns, in 1979, and first published by Dell Magazines, as "Numbers in Place." The game became popular in Japan in 1986, because their alphabet does not lend itself readily to crossword puzzles.

SAY WHAT?

"Flotsam" is that part of a shipwreck that has floated off on its own. "Jetsam" is that which has been intentionally thrown overboard. The distinction was important in the days of yore, as flotsam was property of the Crown and jetsam belonged to the lord whose land it washed up on.

American troops in World War II referred to their life vests as "Mae Wests."

The History of Little Goody Two Shoes was a 1765 fable about a virtuous, poor orphan girl who went through life with one shoe, until one day a rich man gave her a pair of shoes. This led her to later marry a wealthy widower. While the expression "goody two-shoes" first appeared in print a century earlier, this story popularized it.

The word "drunk" has the most synonyms—2,231.

A "scruple" is an apothecary weight equal to twenty grains, or about 1.3 grams.

"BB" gun ammunition is not named for ball bearings, as some believe, but for the BB (double B) size shotgun pellets that the early air gun used.

"Knots" are used to measure nautical speed, because up until the middle of the 1800s, sailors would throw a board tethered to a knotted rope overboard to judge their ship's speed. The rope was knotted every forty-seven feet, three inches. By counting the number of knots that played out in thirty seconds time, as measured on a sand hourglass, an accurate speed was determined. (One knot is equal to 1.151 miles per hour.)

Originally, a "dashboard" was a protective screen placed at the front of a horse-drawn carriage that kept dirt and mud kicked up from dashing horses from soiling the carriage occupants.

"Pneumonoultramicroscopicsilicovolcanoconiosis," a lung disease, is considered the longest word in the English language.

Webster is not only a last name, but also the feminine form of "weaver."

The British word "blimey" is short for "God blind me!"

UM, ER, AH . . .

"Bridges" and "fillers" are words that are used while one collects one's thoughts and searches for the right word.

Some Americans use the word "um" as many as ten to fifteen times an hour while speaking, without realizing it.

Each language has its own all-purpose filler words. For example:

Germans say *oder* or *nicht*.

Japanese lean on the word *nah*. Listeners say *hai*, which means "yes." (They don't say yes in agreement, but to indicate that they hear what the speaker is saying.)

Russians use *znachit*, meaning, "it means." This is similar to the American speech crutch "I mean."

WELL-KNOWN CHARACTERS

A series of random non-alphabet characters used to denote swearing (@#$%&?!) is known as a "grawlix." The term is believed to have been coined by *Beetle Bailey* cartoonist Mort Walker in 1964.

The exclamation point (!) was known as the "note of admiration" until the middle of the 1600s.

The letters "j" and "u" were the last two added to the English alphabet, during the 1500s. Before this, the "i" represented the "j" sound and the "v" represented the "u" sound.

In Britain, a period is known as a "full stop."

MOTHER TONGUES

The Cherokee Indian Sequoyah is the only person in history known to have single-handedly developed an alphabet for an illiterate people. His syllabus, adopted by the Cherokee Nation in 1825, was the first written language for a Native American people.

Basque is said to be the hardest language to learn. It is not related to any other language and has an extremely difficult word structure.

There are more than one thousand different languages spoken on the island nation of New Guinea.

Somalia is the only nation in Africa that has only one language—Somali.

Some African languages use a "click" sound that is made at the same time as other sounds.

ENDNOTES

Reuters news service originally used carrier pigeons to deliver stories.

Singer Carly Simon's father is Richard L. Simon, co-founder of Simon & Schuster.

There really is a Sherwood Forest in England.

The first Christmas cards went on sale in England in 1843. Instead of religious or winter themes, they were illustrated with depictions of fairies, flowers, and other images associated with the coming of spring.

Clifton Hillegass, founder of Cliff's Notes (later Cliffs-Notes), in 1958, intended for them to enrich the reader's appreciation of the classics, not to substitute for actually reading the books. (This may come as a surprise to millions of high school students.)

The highest price ever paid for a book was $8.8 million, in 2000, for a bound set of John Audubon's 1840 work *Birds of America*. The set included 435 hand water-colored plates depicting life-size birds. Separately, the plates sell for $150,000 and up.

Before Charles Dickens came up with the name Tiny Tim, he toyed with the idea of naming the sickly child in *A Christmas Carol* "Puny Pete" or "Small Sam."

The first novel written by a black person to be published in America was Harriet Wilson's *Our Nig*, in 1859.

British publisher Allen Lane popularized the modern paperback in 1935 with the introduction of the Penguin imprint. Booksellers were reluctant to sell paperbacks at the time. It wasn't until Woolworth's successfully moved a large volume of soft covers that other retailers began to stock them.

THIS LAND IS YOUR LAND

READING IS FUNDAMENTAL

The first lending library in America was founded by Benjamin Franklin in Philadelphia in 1731.

About 20 percent of American adults are functionally illiterate. Sixty percent of American prison inmates are illiterate. Worldwide, 1 billion people are illiterate.

Utah has the highest literacy rate in the nation—94 percent.

High school dropouts have a life expectancy 9.2 years lower than graduates.

WHAT'S YOUR MAJOR?

The following are some actual courses being offered at major American colleges:

Philosophy of Star Trek—Georgetown University

Harry Potter Lit—Ohio State University

Video Game Studies—MIT

Tree Climbing—Cornell University

Maple Syrup—Alfred University

Stupidity—Occidental College

Zombies—Ole Miss

Arguing with Judge Judy—Berkeley

STATE-TISTICS

Mountain State
The median age in West Virginia is forty, the oldest of any state.

Evergreen State
Washington leads the country in apple production.

The only rain forest in the continental United States is the Hoh Rain Forest on Washington's Olympic Peninsula.

Empire State
Queens, New York, was established in 1683 and named after Catherine of Braganza, queen consort of Charles II.

New York City hired the first "meter maids" in 1960. They all were women. The first "meter man" was hired in 1967.

The 641-mile-long New York Thruway is the longest toll road in the United States.

The *New York Post* was established in 1801 by Alexander Hamilton as the *New York Evening Post*.

Adirondack Park in upstate New York, at 6 million acres, is larger than Yellowstone, Yosemite, Grand Canyon, Great Smoky, and Everglades National Parks combined.

During the Great Blizzard of 1888 (March 12–14, 1888) forty inches of snow fell on New York City in thirty-six hours and drifts of fifty feet were recorded.

Old Dominion
Virginia's major cash crop is tobacco.

Green Mountain State
The only state capital without a McDonald's is Montpelier, Vermont.

Beehive State
Utah is the state with the highest per capita number of subscribers to adult-content Internet sites. Montana has the fewest subscribers per capita.

Until 1868, Salt Lake City was named Great Salt Lake City.

Lone Star State

The King Ranch in Texas is larger than the state of Rhode Island.

Over the course of its history, Texas has been under the control of six different governments—Spain, France, Mexico, the Republic of Texas, the Confederate States, and the United States.

The Six Flags amusement park company began in Texas and took its name from the six different flags that have flown over the state.

Volunteer State

Tennessee's nickname comes from the War of 1812, when volunteer soldiers from Tennessee fought bravely at the Battle of New Orleans.

Tennessee was the last state to secede from the Union during the Civil War and the first state to be readmitted after the war.

Jack Daniel's Tennessee Whiskey is made in a "dry" county.

Tennessee and Missouri each border eight other states.

Mount Rushmore State

The Crazy Horse Memorial, in the Black Hills of South Dakota, is a mountain carving now in progress. When completed it will be the world's largest sculpture (563 feet high, 641 feet long, carved in the round). It is the focal point of an educational and cultural memorial to and for the North American Indian.

Keystone State

The nation's first daily newspaper, the *Pennsylvania Packet and Daily Advertiser*, began publication in 1784.

The Philadelphia Zoo, which opened in 1874, is America's oldest.

Edwin L. Drake drilled the world's first oil well in Titusville, Pennsylvania, in 1859, creating the modern American petroleum industry.

Kennett Square, Pennsylvania, is acclaimed as the "Mushroom Capital of the World."

Pennsylvania has the most covered bridges of any state—more than two hundred.

The mile marker at the U.S. Interstate 78 exit for Hellertown, Pennsylvania, is 66.6.

Penn State has been voted the top "party school" in the country.

Peach State

In Gainesville, Georgia, the self-proclaimed "Chicken Capital of the World," it is illegal to eat chicken with a fork.

Georgia leads the nation in peanut, pecan, and peach production.

Ocean State

Rhode Island is officially known as Rhode Island and Providence Plantations.

Rhode Island was the first British colony to outlaw slavery, in 1652.

Teenagers in Rhode Island cannot work pumping gas, but girls as young as sixteen can be employed as strippers, as long as they are home by 11:30 p.m.

The White Horse Tavern in Newport, Rhode Island, was established in 1673 and claims to be the oldest operating tavern in America.

Land of 10,000 Lakes

The Minneapolis Skyway System, in Minnesota, is an enclosed climate-controlled pedestrian skywalk system that covers sixty-nine blocks, or seven miles, making it the largest in the world.

Golden State

Modesto, California, is the car theft capital of the nation, with 1419 thefts for every 100,000 residents in 2005.

The largest amphitheater in America is the San Manuel Amphitheater in Devore, California, which seats 65,000.

It is estimated there are approximately 500,000 detectable seismic tremors in California annually.

The temperature has never reached 90°F in Eureka, California, since records have been kept.

Garden State
New Jersey has the densest highway system in the country.

The first Indian reservation in North America was created in New Jersey in 1758, in Indian Mills.

The Union Water Sphere, in Union, New Jersey, is the tallest water sphere in the world, at 212 feet. It holds 250,000 gallons.

Richard Hollingshead opened the first ever drive-in movie theater in Camden, New Jersey, in 1933.

There are six Washington, New Jerseys, and five Franklin, New Jerseys.

Beaver State
Oregon's state flag is the only state flag with different designs on the front and reverse sides.

Sooner State
A Sooner was a settler who jumped the gun by claiming land before the official start of the Indian Territory Land Rush in 1889.

Carl Magee invented the first coin-operated parking meter, which was installed in Oklahoma City on July 16, 1935.

Oklahoma has the largest Indian population of any state—over 250,000.

The name "Oklahoma" literally means "red people," coming from the Choctaw words *okla*, meaning "human," and *homa*, meaning "red."

Buckeye State

The Y-Bridge in Zanesville, Ohio, which spans the confluence of the Muskingum and Licking Rivers, is the only bridge in the nation that one can cross and still be on the same side of the river.

Cincinnati had the first ambulance service and the first professional fire department in the United States.

Cleveland erected America's first traffic light, in 1914.

The cash register was invented by saloon owner James J. Ritty, of Dayton, Ohio, in 1879 to prevent his employees from pilfering the profits.

The first police car was deployed on the streets of Akron in 1899. It ran on electricity.

Peace Garden State

North Dakota grows more sunflowers than any other state.

Tar Heel State

The largest privately owned home in America is Biltmore Estate in Asheville, North Carolina. It encompasses 175,000 square feet with 250 rooms. It is owned by one of the descendants of George Washington Vanderbilt.

North Carolina is the number one state in textile jobs and tobacco production.

Granite State
New Hampshire was the first colony to declare its independence from England, in 1774.

Silver State
Gambling was legalized in Nevada in 1931.

Bugsy Siegel named the Flamingo casino in Las Vegas for his girlfriend, Virginia Hill, who had long, skinny legs.

Las Vegas is home to fifteen of the twenty biggest hotels in the world.

Eighty-six percent of Nevada is land owned by the federal government.

Hoosier State
Ball State University in Muncie, Indiana, was named for the Ball Brothers, of Ball jar fame, who bought the failing Indiana Normal Institute out of foreclosure and donated it to the state.

Bayou State
Louisiana is the only state with a legal system based on the Napoleonic Code. The other forty-nine states have legal systems based on English common law.

In Louisiana, judges base their decisions based on their interpretation of the law, as opposed to legal precedent.

Pine Tree State

Maine only borders on one other state—New Hampshire.

Ninety percent of American lobsters come from Maine.

Bay State

The first American subway system opened in Boston in 1897.

In 1634, Boston Common became the first public park in America.

Martha's Vineyard has a year-round population of about 15,000, but in the summer 100,000 or more people may be on the island.

Wolverine State

There are no wolverines in Michigan.

The largest crucifix in the world is the fifty-five-foot-tall Cross in the Woods in Indian River, Michigan, which was made from a single redwood tree.

Michigan has the longest freshwater shoreline in the world.

Show Me State
Kansas City, Missouri, has more fountains than any city in the world, save Rome.

Gem State
Hell's Canyon in Idaho is the deepest river gorge in America.

Aloha State
One of the Hawaiian Islands, Niihau, has been privately owned by the Robinson family since 1864. The native population is around 160 and the island is off-limits to all outsiders, except a few tour groups and some military personnel.

Diamond Head in Waikiki got its name from British sailors who mistook the calcite in its rocks for diamonds.

Constitution State
In 1901, Connecticut became the first state to set speed limits for autos—12 miles per hour in cities, 15 miles per hour in the country.

Rocky Mountain State/Centennial State
Denver's Colfax Avenue is the longest continuous street in America, at forty miles.

Grand Canyon State
Arizona produces 60 percent of the country's copper.

Last Frontier
Rhode Island could fit into Alaska 379 times.

Juneau, Alaska, is not accessible by car, only by sea or air. All cars in the city arrive by barge or ferry.

First State
Delaware was the first state to ratify the Constitution.

Dover, Delaware, is one of five state capitals not connected to the interstate highway system, the others being Carson City, Nevada; Juneau, Alaska; Jefferson City, Missouri; and Pierre, South Dakota.

Sunshine State
Boca Raton translates to "mouse mouth" in Spanish.

GOD BLESS AMERICA

The first American synagogue, Shearith Israel, was built in New York City in 1730.

On August 24, 1964, the first American Catholic mass in English was celebrated in St. Louis, Missouri.

Elizabeth Ann Bayley Seton was the first native-born American citizen to be canonized.

DAM IT!

There are 845,000 dams in the world. Eighty thousand are in the United States.

Hoover Dam, between Nevada and Arizona, is the country's largest.

Forty-nine dams have failed in the United States between 2000 and 2007.

GIVE ME YOUR TIRED . . .

The Statue of Liberty cost $250,000 to build. The pedestal she stands on cost $334,000. The people of France paid for the statue. Americans paid for the pedestal.

It took so long to raise money for the base that the statue had to be stored in crates for eleven months until the structure could be completed. New York governor Grover Cleveland vetoed a bill passed by the state legislature to donate $50,000 toward the pedestal.

The Statue of Liberty functioned as a lighthouse from 1886 to 1902.

In 1916, the statue was badly damaged when German agents blew up the ammunition depot on neighboring Black Tom Island. Her arm has been closed to visitors ever since.

Liberty Island lies in New Jersey waters but is part of New York.

FATS FOOD NATION

Mississippi is the state with the highest percentage of obese adults—32.5—followed by West Virginia, Alabama, Tennessee, and South Carolina. The least obese states are Colorado, Massachusetts, Connecticut, Rhode Island, and Hawaii.

Huntington, West Virginia, is the fattest and most unhealthful city. Nearly half of adult residents are obese. (The city also leads the nation in rates of diabetes and heart disease. If all that weren't bad enough, half of Huntington's elderly have lost all their teeth.)

Obese Americans, on average, have medical bills that are $1,400 higher per year than non-obese citizens.

The average American eats more than fifty tons of food in a lifetime.

HALLOWED HALLS

The term "ivy" was first used in association with the Ivy League schools in 1933, by *New York Tribune* sportswriter Stanley Woodward.

Seven of the eight Ivy League schools predate the American Revolution. Cornell was founded in 1865.

All the Ivy League schools, except Cornell, were founded by church groups. Princeton University was founded as a school to train Presbyterian ministers, in 1746. Originally located in Elizabeth, New Jersey, and known as the College of New Jersey, the school moved to Princeton in 1756.

Princeton excluded women undergraduates until 1969.

G-MEN

Before the formation of the Federal Bureau of Investigation, the U.S. government hired private detective agencies, such as Pinkertons, to investigate crimes.

The FBI began as the Special Agent Force in 1908. Teddy Roosevelt formed the Force to investigate illegal land sales in the western states.

In 1934, Congress granted FBI agents the right to carry guns, twenty-six years after the Bureau was formed.

The FBI has a database of more than 47 million subjects' fingerprints.

Only 10 percent of those who apply to the FBI are accepted.

WANTED: DEAD OR ALIVE

Bounty hunters are hired by bail bondsmen and work on a commission of about 10 to 20 percent of the total bail bond.

Bounty hunters have greater powers of arrest than do most police. When people sign a bail bond, they agree that they can be arrested by a bail bonds agent and they give up their right of extradition. Bounty hunters can enter private property unannounced and don't need to read a suspect Miranda rights.

Each year, twenty thousand American fugitives are caught by bounty hunters. That's 87 percent of all bail jumpers.

Only Kentucky, Illinois, and Oregon prohibit bounty hunters from making an arrest without a court order.

The United States and the Philippines are the only countries that allow bounty hunting.

JAIL BIRDS

One percent of the American population is in jail.

Each year 14 million Americans get arrested.

One million Americans are arrested for drunkenness every year.

There are currently 142,000 prisoners serving life sentences in the United States.

It costs $60,000 to build a new prison cell in the United States.

It costs about $26,000 a year to maintain the average prisoner.

LOTTO FEVER

The only states that do not have lotteries are Alabama, Alaska, Hawaii, Mississippi, Nevada, Utah, and Wyoming.

The largest lottery prize was a $390 million 2007 MegaMillions jackpot won by one ticket sold in New Jersey and one in Georgia.

SNAIL MAIL

Since 2000, 188,000 of those big blue postal mailboxes have been removed from streets across the country because of declining mail volume, as a result of increased usage of email and online bill paying. Only 176,936 boxes remain.

The *J. W. Westcott II* is the only boat in the United States that delivers mail to other boats that are under way. She is based out of Detroit, Michigan, and brings mail to ships that pass under the Ambassador Bridge on the Detroit River.

RED STATE, BLUE STATE

"Red states" tend to vote for Republican presidential candidates, "blue states" for Democratic candidates. Journalist Tim Russert is responsible, in large part, for this color association. He assigned the colors during his coverage of the 2000 presidential election. Before this, networks used colored maps of the states on election night to indicate which party won which state, but there was no uniformity. Red states are now considered to lean conservative and blue states liberal. "Purple states" are those that can swing either way.

Before 2000, historically, the color red was more often associated with liberal states.

🌰 BLUE DOGS

Blue Dog Democrats are Democratic House members who have moderate to conservative views. They formed a coalition in 1995. The name was taken from the South's longtime description of a party loyalist as one who would vote for a "yellow dog" if it were on the ballot as a Democrat. The "blue" part came from former Texas Democratic House member Pete Green, who quipped that moderates were being "choked blue" by "extreme" left-wing Democrats.

BUYING INFLUENCE

The U.S. Chamber of Commerce is by far the biggest spending lobby group in America. In 2008, they spent $93.6 million in their lobbying efforts. The second-place lobbyist was ExxonMobil, who spent $29 million, followed by AARP at $27.9 million, PG&E at $27.2 million, and Northrop Grumman at $20.7 million. The American Medical Association, the Pharmaceutical Research & Manufacturers of America, and the American Hospital Association followed close behind.

DOCUMENTED IMMIGRANTS

Immigrants to America who came through Ellis Island in the early 1900s had to prove they were free of disease or wait in a hospital until cured, if that was possible. Those with incurable diseases were sent back, as were women traveling alone, or anyone with under twenty dollars, unless a sponsor or family member was there to meet them.

Green cards have not been green since 1964.

Spanning the Globe

COLON AND DONG

The monetary unit of Bolivia is the boliviano. In Venezuela it is the bolívar.

The Vietnamese unit of currency is the dong. In Costa Rica it is the colon.

WELL-SHORN BRIDES

Muslim brides remove all their body hair before the wedding night. They keep their pubic hair off thereafter. Some Muslim men also remove their pubic hair.

Couples in Kuwait have two wedding parties—one for the men and another for the women and children.

GOTTA KEEP 'EM SEPARATED

In Japan there are special train cars just for women, so that they don't get groped. Japanese men now want a special car so that they won't be accused of groping.

RUN-ON SENTENCE

Written Thai is one long, continuous string of closely spaced words, without much punctuation or capitalization.

CHINA DOLLS

Traditionally, Chinese brides have worn a red dress for good luck.

Married women in Korea traditionally wear their hair up in a bun, while single girls prefer pigtails.

Korean women will cover their mouths while laughing.

WHEN IN CHINA

The Chinese have a different sense of personal space from Westerners. They will jostle each other in public settings, as opposed to forming an orderly line.

At a Chinese dinner, it is acceptable to loudly slurp, chew, and burp.

Public spitting is also okay in China. The Chinese feel it is necessary for getting rid of bodily waste.

COLOR MY WORLD

In France, the Netherlands, and Sweden, the color green is associated with toiletries.

White is a funeral color in Japan.

In Brazil and Mexico, purple is the funeral color.

VERY SUPERSTITIOUS

When giving flowers in Europe it is considered unlucky to give an even number, so Europeans give odd numbers, except for thirteen.

In China, Japan, and Korea, the word *shi* means "four" and "death," so the number four is considered unlucky. On the other hand, the word *faat* means "eight" and "prosper," so eight is considered a lucky number.

Marigolds are funeral flowers in Mexico and, as such, shouldn't be used for other occasions.

HOW'S TRICKS?

In Japan, prostitution is illegal, but selling non-coital sex acts is legal.

In Sweden, selling sex is legal, but buying sex is illegal.

Over 1 million children in India are involved in prostitution.

HIPPITY HOP

In parts of Switzerland, it's the Easter Cuckoo, not Bunny, who brings the colored eggs.

> In parts of Australia, the Chocolate Bilby (a bilby is a desert-dwelling marsupial) is competing with the Easter Bunny in popularity. Rabbits are a major pest there, whereas the poor little bilbys are quite endangered.

LUXEMBOURGISH

Luxembourg is the only grand duchy in the world. It is ruled by a grand duke.

> Luxembourg has the highest gross domestic product in the world.

One of the three official languages of Luxembourg is Luxembourgish.

SEA DOG ISLANDS

There are no canaries in the Canary Islands. Their name derives from the Latin *canis*, or "dog." The first Romans who visited the islands were struck by the many monk seals, or sea dogs, they found there. This ancient connection lives on today through the two dogs found on the islands' coat of arms.

PACKAGE DEAL

When a Todan woman in southern India married a man, she also got all of his brothers.

RAW DEAL

During times of severe drought in the eastern India region of Bihar, farmers have their unmarried daughters plow the fields in the nude, while chanting hymns, in order to embarrass the weather gods into making it rain.

EATING CROW

In Lithuania, men eat crow meat to increase their sexual potency.

GLOBAL WARMING?

Two glaciers in the Patagonian Alps of Argentina and Peru are growing, instead of shrinking like others in the area.

NOW YOU SEE IT . . .

Beloye Lake, about 155 miles east of Moscow, disappeared overnight in 2005, when its water was sucked into a cave beneath it.

WORLD LEADERS

Germany is the world leader in solar power production.

The King Fahd International Airport, in Saudi Arabia, is the world's largest, with a land size of 780 square kilometers. It is larger than the country of Bahrain.

China is by far the world's leading grower of tobacco, producing more than five times the crop of the United States. India and Brazil are numbers two and three. The United States is number four.

People in China eat three hundred to four hundred pounds of rice a year, Americans about eight.

According to a 2006 study, the Danes profess themselves to be the most "content" people.

Workers in Brazil and Lithuania get a whopping forty-one paid days off each year.

IF AT FIRST YOU DON'T SUCCEED

A sixty-eight-year-old South Korean woman finally passed her written driver's test in November 2009, after taking it 950 times. She only needed a score of 60 percent to pass. (Now it's on to the road test.)

WATER RETENTION

The Three Gorges Dam in China will be the biggest in the world when completed. Its projected cost is $25 billion and its 410-mile-long reservoir will have displaced 1.3 million people.

Sixty-five percent of all the freshwater in the world that is bound for the ocean is impeded by dams.

COUNTRY CONFUSION

Holland is a part of the Netherlands. "Dutch" refers to inhabitants of the Netherlands, not just Holland.

Taiwan is not considered a country by most other countries.

Not counting Taiwan, there are 194 countries in the world.

Seven new countries were formed when Yugoslavia broke up—Bosnia and Herzegovina, Croatia, Kosovo, Macedonia, Montenegro, Serbia, and Slovenia.

Fourteen nations were created when the Soviet Union dissolved.

The United States has fourteen territories; Britain has fifteen; and France has sixteen.

Greenland is also known as *Kalaallit Nunaat*. It is in North America, but is part of the Kingdom of Denmark.

NATIONS UNITED

One hundred and ninety-two countries belong to the United Nations. Taiwan, Kosovo, and Vatican City do not.

Switzerland did not join the UN until 2002, because of the whole neutrality thing.

DATING DECORUM

In Japan and Korea, most teens don't start dating until after high school. It is the boy's job to ask the girl out and to pay. In Australia, girls often do the asking out and paying.

DO YOU BELIEVE?

In days of yore, superstitious folk believed that witches used children's teeth to cast spells. In England, they burned a child's tooth when it fell out. In other counties the teeth were buried. In the twentieth century, people started hiding children's teeth under a pillow for the tooth fairy.

A children's story called "The Tooth Fairy," by Lee Rogow, was published in 1949, and the fairy became widely known in the 1950s. Today, many countries have their own unique versions of this odd custom. The following is a short list of some practices around the world:

Japan and Korea—They throw a lower tooth on the roof and an upper tooth under the house. This is done so the new upper tooth grows downward and the lower tooth grows upward.

Austria—The tooth is made into a pendant or key chain; or the upper tooth is thrown under the house and the lower tooth is thrown over the house.

France—The tooth goes under the pillow and the fairy leaves a gift, not money.

Italy—They save the teeth as a keepsake.

Mexico and Spain—A mouse is said to take the tooth from under the pillow and leaves money.

Mongolia—The tooth is fed to a dog, which is thought of as a guardian angel, so a healthy new tooth will grow.

CHEW ON THIS

Many people in West Africa chew the bitter cola nut for its stimulating and euphoria-producing effects. It also eases hunger pangs.

Cultures in East Africa and Arabia chew the leaves of khat, an evergreen shrub that produces effects similar to those of the cola nut when chewed.

Folks in Bolivia, Peru, and Venezuela chew coca leaves to ease pain and ward off hunger, thirst, and fatigue. Coca extract can also be found in toothpastes and teas in these and other South American countries. Venezuelan president Hugo Chávez says that he chews coca leaves every day. (That explains a lot.)

OIL MOVERS AND SHEIKERS

OPEC (the Organization of Petroleum Exporting Countries) was founded in 1960 by Iran, Iraq, Kuwait, Saudi

Arabia, and Venezuela. Algeria, Angola, Ecuador, Libya, Nigeria, Qatar, and the United Arab Emirates are now also members.

IT'S LIKE THOSE BRITISH HAVE A DIFFERENT WORD FOR EVERYTHING

While America and England share a common language, the Brits have different words for many things. A brief list, with the American word and the British version, follows:

truck—lorry

car trunk—boot

car hood—bonnet

elevator—lift

closet—cupboard

can—tin

letter "z" ("zee")—zed

fanny—a woman's genitalia

chin—pecker

eraser—rubber

drunk—pissed

to bomb—to succeed

homely—homelike, meaning warm and comfortable

drugstore—chemist

vacuum—hoover

nipple—woman's nipple only, not rubber baby bottle nipple, which is called a teat

AN EYE FOR AN EYE

One hundred and two people were beheaded in Saudi Arabia in 2008.

The rules for stoning are codified in Iranian law and are very specific. Article 104 defines the size of the stones and stipulates that "the stones should not be so large that the person dies upon being hit by one or two of them, neither should they be so small that they cannot be called a stone."

WAR, WHAT IS IT GOOD FOR?

The Dahomey Amazons were an all-female fighting unit in the eighteenth and nineteenth centuries in the African nation of Dahomey (now Benin). At one point, they comprised one-third of the country's military. They would oil their bodies before combat to increase evasiveness.

The Battle of New Orleans was fought two weeks after the War of 1812 ended. News that the war was over had not reached the combatants in time.

Antietam was the bloodiest single-day battle in American history. There were 23,000 combined Union and Confederate casualities.

The Thirty Years War (1618–1648) had the forced conversion of Bohemians to Catholicism as its root, but it was triggered when Emperor Ferdinand's envoys were thrown out of a window of the Prague Castle and only survived the fall because the moat was filled with dried manure. This act became known as the Defenestration of Prague.

After almost two hundred years, the Buckingham Palace Guardsmen hats are being switched from North American black bear fur to something synthetic. Each hat takes the skin of an entire bear to make. The eighteen-inch-high hats were first adopted after the battle of Waterloo, to make the soldiers look taller and more intimidating.

In the sixteenth century there were no standing armies. All soldiers were mercenaries.

When the Spanish warships invading Amsterdam in the winter of 1571–72 became frozen in the harbor, the Dutch Army used skates with metal blades to easily outmaneuver and defeat them.

Two Italian city-states went to war in 1325, after troops from Modena stole a wooden bucket from Bologna, killing hundreds of citizens in the process. The resulting war lasted twelve years. The bucket was never returned, and resides today in the Duomo di Modena cathedral bell tower.

The Persian army of 2,500 years ago would use live cats as shields on the front line when fighting the Egyptians, who revered felines and were forbidden by law to kill them, under penalty of death.

The Pontifical Swiss Guard is the oldest military unit in the world. Founded in 1506, their sole job is to protect the pope.

The term "atomic bomb" was first coined by science fiction writer H. G. Wells in his 1914 novel *The World Set Free*. While his book predated nukes by thirty years, he realized the potential decaying atoms had for limitless energy. Wells's fictional atomic bomb was only as powerful as conventional bombs of the time but would continue to explode for days on end.

The unluckiest (or luckiest) man of the twentieth century may have been one Tsutomu Yamaguchi. He was in Hiroshima on a business trip on August 6, 1945, the day the atomic bomb was dropped. Badly injured, he managed to return home to Nagasaki in time for the second blast there three days later. He finally passed away January 4, 2010, at the age of ninety-three.

The Russian MiG aircraft get their name from the names of the two men who founded the bureau that designed them— Artem Mikoyan and Mikhail Gurevich. All versions of MiG fighter planes are denoted with odd numbers.

In the old days, marksmen would hone their skills by shooting snipe (wading birds), hence the term "sniper."

BOOM!

Since 1945, there have been 2,045 nuclear explosions, half of them detonated by the United States.

Saint Barbara, of Santa Barbara fame, is the patron saint of artillerymen and anyone working with explosives.

AGENT ORANGE

More than 21 million gallons of the defoliant Agent Orange were sprayed over South Vietnam during the Vietnam War. According to the government of Vietnam, 4.8 million Vietnamese were exposed to Agent Orange, resulting in 400,000 deaths and disabilities and 500,000 children born with birth defects.

Agent Orange got its name from the orange-striped fifty-five-gallon drums it was shipped in.

The U.S. military also used the chemical Agents Blue, White, Purple, Pink, and Green as defoliants over South Vietnam.

YOU THINK *YOUR* JOB SUCKS

The following are some odd jobs in the days of yore:

A knocker-up, or knocker-upper, was someone in England and Ireland who was paid to wake up clients at a requested hour, so that they would get to work on time. Before the age of alarm clocks and wake-up calls, this service was very useful. The knocker-upper would rap on the window of a client until the client was roused.

From Roman to medieval times, fullers would walk around up to their ankles in vats of stale urine and wool to soften it and tighten up its fibers. Pee was collected from pots on street corners and from schools for this purpose.

Another odd medieval job was arming squire. These lads of between twelve and eighteen put in five-year apprenticeships of running unprotected onto the field of battle to replace broken armor on their knight. After the battle, they were expected to clean the suit of armor of mud, blood, and excreta, using sand, vinegar, and urine to make it shine.

Scottish women in medieval times could earn a living by wading into marshy waters and collecting the leeches that attached to their bare legs.

The groom of the stool was a gentleman in Tudor England whose job it was to attend to the cleaning of the king's backside after a bowel movement. He also was responsible for giving his majesty enemas and laxatives.

There are still nitpickers working in the United States today. Their job is to pick lice and their eggs from the head by examining the root of each hair for infestation.

Link-boys were employed in England in the days before streetlights to escort people home at night with a flaming torch.

Tanners used to soak animal hides in dog and chicken excrement to soften it. Some folks made a living running around city streets scooping up the dog poop. They were known as "pure" collectors.

OF HUMAN BONDAGE

Slaves destined for the New World were captured in raids by other Africans, who traded them for goods with the Europeans.

The transatlantic slave trade ended shortly after the American Revolution.

Ten percent of the African slaves shipped to the New World died in transit.

In total, some 12.4 million Africans were sent to the New World. About 645,000 of them were destined for what is now the United States.

More than half of the European immigrants to America during the 1600s and 1700s arrived as indentured servants. They were required to work for their employer for a period of three to seven years, in exchange for food, lodging, and clothing.

LEE-JACKSON-KING DAY

Between 1984 and 2000, Virginia observed a Lee-Jackson-King Day. This inexplicably incongruous holiday honored Confederate generals Robert E. Lee and Stonewall Jackson, along with civil rights activist Martin Luther King Jr. Virginians still observe Lee-Jackson Day, when all state offices are closed, on the Friday before Martin Luther King Jr. Day.

IS THAT LEGAL?

In early English law, first time offenders could claim something called "benefit of the clergy." Originally for clergy only, but later extended to anyone who was literate, this legal loophole moved one's trial from a criminal court to an ecclesiastical court. Simply by reading a passage from the Bible, typically Psalm 51, and doing penance, even murderers could get an acquittal.

Americans thought for some time that bathing was unhealthful. As late as 1845, the city of Boston forbade bathing, except as directed by a doctor.

Alabama was the first state to legally recognize Christmas, in 1836.

Susan B. Anthony was fined two hundred dollars for voting in the 1872 presidential election. She never paid.

DEEP THROAT

William Mark Felt Sr. was assistant associate director of the FBI in 1972 and also "Deep Throat," the person who supplied *Washington Post* reporter Bob Woodward with information regarding the Watergate break-ins that led to the downfall of President Richard Nixon. Felt adamantly denied that he was Deep Throat until 2005.

Felt had been passed over by Nixon to become the head of the FBI.

Ironically, Felt was convicted, in 1980, of approving break-ins and illegal wiretapping of Weather Underground terrorist members in 1972 and 1973. Ronald Reagan later pardoned him.

THE BRITISH ARE COMING!

Paul Revere didn't shout out, "The British are coming!" during his famous midnight ride. Most people at the time *were* British. He actually yelled, "The regulars are coming out!"

THE BIG DIG

When the United States began planning to build the Panama Canal, routing it through Nicaragua was considered. A lobbying effort by a French group that held vast land holdings in Panama convinced Congress to choose the Panama option. Recently printed stamps from Nicaragua, showing erupting volcanoes, were mailed to all U.S. senators, convincing them of the danger of building the canal in that country. However, there were in fact no active volcanoes anywhere near the canal's proposed path.

JANE ROE

The name John Doe has been used for anonymous court defendants since 1659 in England. A female defendant is known as Jane Doe. Anonymous plaintiffs are known as Richard Roe and Jane Roe. The 1973 Supreme Court abortion case, *Roe v. Wade*, gets half its name from the anonymous woman who brought the case—Jane Roe.

Her real name was Norma L. McCorvey. McCorvey brought suit against the state of Texas, represented by Dallas County District Attorney Henry Wade, arguing for her right to an abortion. McCorvey originally claimed that she had been raped, but later recanted that story.

OH! THE HUMANITY!

The *Hindenburg* airship was forced to use highly flammable hydrogen gas because America controlled the major world supply of the much safer helium and considered it strategically important that the Germans not get any.

Smoking on the *Hindenburg* was actually permitted, in a special smoking lounge. Smokers were furnished with water-filled ashtrays and stewards watched carefully to make sure no ashes went astray.

The exact spot where the zeppelin burned is marked on the ground by a memorial at Lakehurst Naval Air Station (now called Navy Lakehurst) and tours are offered. Foreign nationals are prohibited from the tours for security reasons.

🌰 BIG BOATS

The *Titanic* was one of three huge sister ships built by the White Star Line, the others being the *Olympic* and the *Britannic*.

The *Olympic* was the first of the three to be launched and was captained by Edward Smith. On September 11, 1911, with Smith at the helm, the *Olympic* struck the British warship HMS *Hawke* and was badly damaged. The Royal Navy found the *Olympic* to be at fault. Seven months later, Smith was captain of the ill-fated *Titanic* when it hit the iceberg and sank.

The *Britannic* was the third, and largest, of the sister ships built. It was supposed to be called the *Gigantic*, but the name was changed after the *Titanic* disaster. Like its sisters, the *Britannic* was not very lucky. It was used as a hospital ship in World War I and sank after hitting a mine off the coast of Greece in 1916.

FIRST PETS

Pauline, President Taft's pet cow, was the last to give milk at the White House, from 1910 to 1913.

James Buchanan had a herd of elephants.

Abe Lincoln kept his pet pig at the White House.

Calvin Coolidge had a large menagerie of pets, including a hippo, a wallaby, a raccoon, a bear, and some lion cubs.

Teddy Roosevelt had many pets, among them a one-legged chicken and a badger named Josiah that would nip at the heels of White House guests.

Woodrow Wilson kept a flock of sheep on the White House lawn to free up the groundskeepers for more important work during World War I.

John Adams received an alligator from the Marquis de Lafayette as a gift.

EXECUTIVE NOTES

John Quincy Adams was the only president who lost the popular and Electoral College vote but was still elected. None of the candidates had a majority of the popular or electoral vote in that election, so it was decided in the House of Representatives. Even though challenger Andrew Jackson had a plurality in the popular and electoral vote, they seated Adams.

The first woman to run for president of the United States was Victoria Woodhull, for the Equal Rights Party, in 1872.

Rutherford B. Hayes's wife, Lucy, had him ban alcohol, dancing, card playing, and smoking from the White House.

Ronald Reagan won every state in his 1984 win over Walter Mondale, except Minnesota (and the District of Columbia).

HAIL TO THE CHIEF

In 1870, President Ulysses S. Grant tried to annex the Dominican Republic. He took his idea to the Senate, who voted against the plan.

Ulysses S. Grant once got a ticket and a twenty-dollar fine for riding his horse too fast.

Since George Washington's teeth were so bad, he made sure his horses' teeth were brushed daily.

James Monroe was shot in the shoulder during the Revolutionary War. The musket ball was never removed.

John Quincy Adams served in the Congress after his presidency.

Two of tenth president John Tyler's grandchildren are still alive as of 2009.

Zachary Taylor never voted in a presidential election.

James Buchanan was farsighted in one eye and nearsighted in the other. For this reason, he alternated opening and closing each eye.

Abraham Lincoln worked as a credit reporting correspondent for Dun & Bradstreet, helping to determine the creditworthiness of those he investigated.

Andrew Johnson never went to school. He taught himself to read and write.

Grover Cleveland had a rubber jawbone installed after part of his was removed with cancer.

Benjamin Harrison was so surly that his nickname was the "human iceberg."

Teddy Roosevelt once killed a mountain lion with a knife.

Harry Truman had read all two thousand books in his public library by the time he graduated high school.

Richard Nixon applied to the FBI but was rejected. (The qualifications to be president are apparently less stringent.)

Gerald Ford was shot at *twice* in September 1975, by two different women—Lynette "Squeaky" Fromme and Sara Jane Moore.

James Garfield was shot on July 2, 1881, and died on September 19, 1881. He might have lived, had the doctors been able to locate the bullet in his body. Alexander Graham Bell invented a metal detecting device just to help save the president. The only problem was, the machine worked during tests but did not work on Garfield. Unfortunately, Bell didn't realize that the president's mattress had metal coil springs (which were new at the time) that rendered the device ineffective.

Ronald Reagan had three and a half tons of red, white, and blue jelly beans at his inauguration. That's 2.8 million jelly beans.

Barbara Bush was born Barbara Pierce. She is a direct descendant of Franklin Pierce.

Abraham Lincoln was not born in Illinois, "The Land of Lincoln," but Ronald Reagan was.

Mary Todd Lincoln dated Abe's chief rival—Stephen Douglas—before hooking up with Lincoln.

Shortly before John Wilkes Booth assassinated Abraham Lincoln, a wild coincidence occurred in Jersey City, New Jersey. Famous actor Edwin T. Booth, John Wilkes's brother, saved Lincoln's son, Robert Todd Lincoln, when the latter had slipped off the platform at a railway station near a moving train and was pulled to safety.

In 1826, just before his death, Thomas Jefferson's finances were in such a bad state that he authorized a lottery, with his land holdings as the prize. The scheme never reached fruition.

While Grover Cleveland served as the sheriff of Erie County, New York, he personally hanged two men.

Bill Clinton is allergic to beef, milk, and cat dander.

I CHALLENGE YOU TO A DUEL

Aaron Burr challenged Alexander Hamilton to a duel after Hamilton insulted him at a dinner party. The two were bitter New York State political rivals.

Aaron Burr was vice president of the United States when he killed Hamilton in the 1804 duel, just across the Hudson River from Manhattan in Weehawken, New Jersey.

Dueling was illegal in New York and New Jersey at the time, but the penalty was death in New York and somewhat less severe in New Jersey. Burr was charged with murder in both states, but all the charges were eventually dropped and he served out his term as vice president.

Hamilton had previously challenged James Monroe to a duel, in 1796, when Hamilton mistakenly believed that Monroe had made public an extramarital affair Hamilton was having. Ironically, it was Aaron Burr who persuaded Hamilton that Monroe was not responsible, and the duel was canceled.

The ill-tempered Hamilton challenged many others to duels in his lifetime.

Alexander Hamilton's oldest son, Philip, died in a duel in 1801, three years before Hamilton.

SURVEY SAYS . . .

George Gallup took the first known poll in history when, as the editor of the newspaper at the University of Iowa in the early 1920s, he conducted a survey to find the prettiest girl on campus. Gallup ended up marrying the winner, Ophelia Smith.

TREND STARTERS

Go-go dancing originated at the Peppermint Lounge in New York when young women began to do the twist on tabletops in the early 1960s.

The idea of "dropping" a ball to mark time (as on New Year's Eve) goes back to 1833, when England's Royal Observatory in Greenwich did so at precisely 1 p.m. each day, so sea captains could set their chronometers.

The first European executed in the American colonies was John Billington. In 1640, he was hung for murder in the Plymouth Colony.

The crossing of one's fingers for luck dates back to the time of the persecution of early Christians. Fearing for their safety if they openly crossed themselves in public, they did so furtively, with their fingers.

TALES OF THE SEA

The Pilgrims originally set sail on two ships—the *Mayflower* and the *Speedwell*. However, the *Speedwell* began to leak, so both ships turned back and only the *Mayflower* later went to America.

No women were allowed on Columbus's first two trips to the New World. On the third, one woman was allowed for every ten men.

Ship commander William Bligh was only a lieutenant at the time of the mutiny on the *Bounty*, in 1789.

ONWARD CHRISTIAN SOLDIERS

The Salvation Army is a Christian church that is organized like a military service. Members have ranks and wear uniforms. Much of their early good works involved getting people to stop drinking alcohol. In England, they were opposed by another "army"—the "Skeleton Army"—made up of tavern owners who actually attacked Salvation Army meetings in 1884 by throwing rocks, eggs, rats, and tar at their members.

STONE COLD KILLERS

Lee Harvey Oswald

According to the Warren Commission, on April 10, 1963, months before assassinating John F. Kennedy, Lee Harvey Oswald attempted to assassinate retired Major General Edwin Walker. He fired a rifle shot at the general as he sat in his Dallas dining room. The bullet narrowly missed, but Walker was injured by bullet fragments.

It is very likely that the rifle used to shoot at Walker was the same one that later killed John F. Kennedy, on November 22, 1963.

Oswald died in the same hospital that Kennedy had two days earlier, after he was shot by Jack Ruby.

In 1981, Oswald's body was exhumed after a British writer claimed that the man who shot Kennedy was not Oswald, but a Soviet body double who was really a KGB assassin. Dental analysis quickly debunked this theory.

Sirhan Sirhan

After Sirhan Bishara Sirhan assassinated Robert Kennedy, on June 5, 1968, in the Ambassador Hotel in Los Angeles, he was subdued by some of Kennedy's supporters, including author George Plimpton, football star Rosie Grier, and Olympic champion Rafer Johnson.

Five other people were wounded during the shooting. All later recovered.

Sirhan is believed to have killed Kennedy because of the senator's support of Israel in the Six Days War, which had started exactly one year to the day before the assassination.

Sirhan was sentenced to death in the gas chamber in 1969, but this sentence was later commuted when California suspended capital punishment in 1972. He is still serving out his life sentence.

James Earl Ray

Martin Luther King's assassin, Ray was serving a twenty-year sentence for armed robbery in 1967 when he escaped by hiding in a truck transporting baked goods from the prison.

He was captured two months after the April 4, 1968, assassination, at London's Heathrow Airport, when he raised suspicions by carrying two different Canadian passports.

Ray pleaded guilty to murder so as to avoid a trial and a potential sentence of death by electrocution, receiving ninety-nine years instead.

He later recanted his confession and insisted that his brother and another man were responsible, not him.

In 1977, Ray again escaped from prison in Tennessee, but was recaptured three days later, for which he had an additional year added to his sentence.

He died in 1998, from kidney disease caused by hepatitis C that he probably contracted from a blood transfusion he received after being stabbed while in prison.

John Hinckley Jr.

John Hinckley Jr., who attempted to kill Ronald Reagan on March 11, 1981, was obsessed with Jodie Foster and thought that becoming a historical figure would put him on an equal footing with her. He called his attempt "the greatest love offering in the history of the world."

Hinckley first considered hijacking a plane and killing himself, but later stalked President Jimmy Carter, until he was arrested on firearms charges.

He hit Reagan with a bullet that ricocheted off the president's limo and wounded three others.

Hinckley was found not guilty by reason of insanity and sent to a mental hospital.

The verdict so enraged the general public that several states later repealed the option of an insanity defense.

Hinckley now gets nine day visits with his mother a year and can even get a driver's license.

Mark David Chapman

Mark David Chapman, who killed John Lennon outside New York's Dakota Hotel on December 8, 1980, had earlier tried to kill himself by running a vacuum hose from his car's tailpipe inside the vehicle. The attempt failed when the hose melted.

In October 1980, Chapman went to Manhattan to kill Lennon but, after watching the movie *Ordinary People*, changed his mind.

Chapman later apparently became very mad at Lennon for saying that he didn't believe in God or the Beatles.

On the day of the murder, he staked out the entrance to the Dakota with others wishing to see Lennon and actually met John and Yoko Ono leaving the building, getting them to sign an album and pose for a photo. Not content with this, he waited for them to return later in the evening and gunned down Lennon.

After the shooting, Chapman sat down and read *The Catcher in the Rye*, a book with which he was obsessed, until police arrived to arrest him.

He was sentenced to twenty years to life and remains incarcerated in Attica State Prison in New York, where he is allowed two conjugal visits from his wife each year.

WHAT GENEVA CONVENTION?

Human rights are a modern notion. Below are a few examples of tortures used in the past:

Henry VIII once demanded that a cook convicted of murder be slowly boiled in one of his own pots. In the days of yore, a person was boiled alive in a large metal cauldron filled with cold water up to the neck. A fire was lit below and the water temperature increased slowly to inflict as much pain as possible.

Dunking was a popular method to extract a confession. The accused was chained to a chair and dunked in cold water for progressively longer periods of time. (Sound familiar?)

Torture with water also involved putting a funnel in the victim's mouth and progressively pouring larger quantities of water into the stomach. Inquisitors liked this method since it didn't leave any marks on the body.

A person could be locked into the stocks barefooted so passersby could tickle their soles. One diabolical twist was rubbing honey on the bare feet and encouraging an animal to lick them for hours on end. Some people may actually have died laughing.

The rack is said to have been the most effective torture device of all time.

In Old England and Scotland, women could be gagged for the offense of gossiping. The law did not apply to men, who could be as obnoxious as they liked.

A gossip was sometimes punished with the branks, a metal cage that fit over the head, with a metal plate that was placed on top of the tongue to prevent speaking.

WHEN JUST DEATH IS NOT ENOUGH

Starting in the middle of the thirteenth century and lasting until the end of the eighteenth century, men convicted of treason in England were drawn and quartered. Women, on the other hand, were burned at the stake, until 1790.

Isaac Newton was master of the Royal Mint from 1699 to 1727 and as such had many counterfeiters hung and drawn and quartered.

Many famous executed persons had their heads adorn poles on the south gate of London Bridge, the first being

William Wallace of Scotland, of *Braveheart* fame, in 1305. Sir Thomas More and Thomas Cromwell also had their heads grace London Bridge.

A gibbet is an iron cage shaped like the human body where executed criminals would be publicly displayed. The last two men to be gibbeted were given the honor in England in 1832.

ACKNOWLEDGMENTS

I'd like to thank my wonderful editor, Jeanette Shaw, for her guiding hand and for giving me free rein to come up with the most perfectly useless information that I can unearth. It's always a lot of fun! I am also grateful to Rick Willet and Emma Hinkle for their most thorough fact-checking and Bryan Landsberg for designing the cutest cover in the series. Many thanks also to a super literary agent, Janet Rosen.

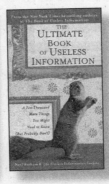